CHAMPIONS AGAIN

Champions
A G A I N

BRYAN ROBSON
WITH TOM TYRRELL

PARTRIDGE PRESS

LONDON · NEW YORK · TORONTO · SYDNEY · AUCKLAND

TRANSWORLD PUBLISHERS LTD
61–63 Uxbridge Road, London W5 5SA

TRANSWORLD PUBLISHERS (AUSTRALIA) PTY LTD
15–25 Helles Avenue, Moorebank, NSW 2170

TRANSWORLD PUBLISHERS (NZ) LTD
3 William Pickering Drive, Albany, Auckland

Published 1993 by Partridge Press
a division of Transworld Publishers Ltd
Copyright © Bryan Robson and Tom Tyrrell

A catalogue record for this book is available from the British Library.

ISBN 1 85225 238 3

Typeset in 11pt Monotype Times New Roman
by Phoenix Typesetting, Ilkley, West Yorkshire.

Printed in Great Britain by
Mackays of Chatham PLC, Chatham, Kent.

This book is dedicated to all my family who have given
me support during my career at Manchester United.

CHAMPIONS AGAIN

CONTENTS

CHAPTER ONE

A Champion Summer

IT WAS THE BEST SUMMER I CAN REMEMBER, EVEN THOUGH IT WAS probably one of the wettest on record. To be honest it could have been knee-deep in snow for all we cared, things would still have seemed glorious.

I don't know when the summer of 1993 was officially due to start but as far as I am concerned it began on Monday 3 May. It was the day the clouds lifted and the sun came into the lives of everybody connected with Manchester United.

That morning I made a dash to pick up the papers to make sure that it had not been a dream. There it was on the front and back pages of every newspaper, the headlines I had waited such a long time to read:

'Champions! United have done it.'

'Fergie takes the title.'

'Villa slip to end United's 26-year wait.'

Big bold letters topped the story of our championship success. We had done it. Manchester United were at the top of the tree, the winners of the FA Premier League.

In the city itself it was a quiet Bank Holiday. Many of the shops were closed but there was something special in the air. It reminded me of the sort of feeling we must all have experienced as children, waking up on Christmas morning and wondering what treats might lie ahead.

Everyone I spoke to, neighbours passing on their morning walk, friends on the phone, seemed excited, as if they were getting ready for a celebration.

In truth it was really only the United fans who were celebrating, and by mid-morning they were out in their thousands waiting for the pubs to open, as the off-licences did brisk business. If you happened to support any other team you kept a low profile, or joined in the fun with your Red neighbours – the drinks were on them!

Fans flocked to Old Trafford where that night we were due to play our last home game of the season. They got there hours before the kick-off standing in groups, laughing and chatting their way through their own stories of the season.

They were happy to wait for the game. We had ended an even longer wait. We had bridged a 26-year gap from the time Sir Matt Busby's side last took the title and I was so proud to be part of the team that did it. Alex Ferguson had become the first manager since the great man to lead United to the top and he was justifiably proud.

The excitement had been killed a little because Oldham had beaten Aston Villa the previous afternoon, meaning that Ron Atkinson's side could no longer catch us. It had become a two-horse race between us and Villa after Norwich slipped off the pace. When Latics, who were fighting to stay up, won at Villa Park that was that, we were out of reach.

So we were already champions before we kicked off against Blackburn Rovers. But who cared?

I spent most of the day trying to relax but the phone never stopped. There were congratulatory calls from relatives, friends and neighbours, and demands for interviews from the media.

By the time I got to Old Trafford for the pre-match meal the place was awash with supporters. They were packed onto the fore-court, jumping around chanting and singing and pressing their faces against the car windows as I drove up. There were banners every-where and the people selling them in the streets were raking it in.

As we chatted in the dressing room before the match it was obvious that the adrenalin wasn't flowing the way it usually did. There were no signs of any nerves – none of those little twinges you get in your stomach even after all my time in the game. The other lads were the same, laughing and smiling. No signs of any tension. Everybody was totally relaxed as if we were rolling up for a training session.

There we were getting ready for one of the most important games in the club's history, but because of the circumstances we were able to treat it like a friendly. I know it would have been a different story if we had needed to take three points from Blackburn to win the championship. But the pressure was off and you could tell by the effect it had on everybody.

Nothing could take away the title, it was ours.

We could hear the crowd as we changed and when we ran out for the warm-up it was like going to a massive carnival. The supporters were having a party.

It was party time for us too. To tell the truth the party had been going on for 24 hours.

For the record we beat Blackburn 3–1 although it took us a little while to settle. We were a goal down before we really got things going. Then the lads turned it on and many saw it as a fitting way to mark the occasion. Ryan Giggs bent a free kick beyond the reach of Bobby Mimms to level the scores as I sat and watched things from the sub's bench.

The gaffer told me to warm up a bit just before half time, then at the break pulled Lee Sharpe off and sent me out for the second half. I wanted to play and the crowd gave me a great welcome, but I wasn't surprised that Lee came off. I think he was still feeling the effects of the night before.

Eric Cantona weaved a bit of his French magic for Paul Ince to put us ahead, then in the last minute Gary Pallister took a free kick and smacked the ball through the wall. That was that. Never mind the Oldham result, we had done the job ourselves.

My feeling of pride was tremendous. I was so grateful to have been a part of the side which now linked the team of the 1990s to the days of Law, Best and Charlton.

I know they were legends to the supporters and world-class players, but there were times when their success seemed like a great cloud hanging over us. Their achievements had haunted everyone who had pulled on a United shirt for more than a quarter of a century.

No matter what had been won during that time there were always those critics who would chip in: 'Fine. But when are you going to win the championship?'

That was behind us now. We could all look to the future.

As the referee blew the final whistle I prepared myself for what had to be my proudest moment in football, knowing a weight had gone from our shoulders. A few small steps but giant strides for Bryan Robson. I knew that it could be one of the final milestones in my playing career so it was something I wanted to enjoy to the full.

I was going up to collect the Premier League trophy, and if this was to be the last trophy I would collect then it was certainly the most important.

Some folks will say I've been lucky, that I have had my fair share of success. Three times I have climbed those steps to the Royal Box at Wembley and been handed the FA Cup and I know what a thrill that is, but it was overshadowed by the feeling of pride as I walked towards the presentation rostrum at Old Trafford.

I suppose the fact that it was all happening in our own stadium had a lot to do with it. So many prizes are won on neutral grounds, but not this time. Manchester United were receiving the biggest prize the domestic game has to offer in front of our own supporters. That was special.

There was something unique in the presentation itself. Not only was it the first time the new trophy had been handed over but there were two of us going to collect it. I had my doubts that I would be involved, but before the kick-off the manager had pulled me to one side and told me that he wanted both Steve Bruce and me to go up for the trophy. I was delighted.

Although I was club captain I had been out for most of the season with a variety of injuries. Brucie had skippered the side for virtually every game, and while I was given the armband whenever I played, because he had started the game that night and I had been on the bench, I was sure he would be the one to pick up the trophy.

It would not have been the end of the world if the boss had said that Steve would lead the way, but no, we went up together and I thought it was a great gesture.

The manager said that it was in recognition of all my years at the club . . . Brucie reckoned it was to stop me moaning!

The handshakes, hugs and pats on the back came from every quarter. We pushed our way through the crowd and I was surprised Steve and I were able to climb the few steps, let alone play in such a vital game, when I thought back to the party we had the night before.

It was the sort of get-together that would have earned everybody a rocket and a club fine if it had happened at any other time in the season. There we were on the eve of what days earlier had been seen as one of the most important games in the history of Manchester United, knocking back the booze and still hard at it well past our normal curfew time.

I don't mean just a couple of us, but the whole squad!

When the news came through that Oldham had beaten Villa my telephone was red hot. Every call was an invitation from somebody to go for a drink. Reluctantly I turned them down until Steve rang.

I wasn't sure what to do. We had a game the next day . . . But what the heck, we were the champions, so Denise and I decided we would go when we were invited round. Just a quiet drink, the 4 of us together. That's what I thought.

By the time we got there the rest of the lads were already arriving. Steve had invited the lot – players, wives, girlfriends, they all turned up. It was party time at the Bruces and what a time we had.

There must have been a few sore heads the next morning, but they say that the best cure for a hangover is another quick slurp, so after we had done the business against Blackburn we were ready for another session.

First we strolled round the Old Trafford pitch on a lap of honour. The noise was deafening, beyond anything I had experienced there before. A wall of sound hit us as we stared into a sea of faces looking for family and friends. It was impossible to make out individuals, everyone merged into a red and white mass. They were ecstatic, singing their heads off. We were the champions.

We all found ourselves being swept along in the emotion, joining in the songs and chants, collecting scarves, flags and hats from the fans and we stayed out on the pitch for ages. Eventually we forced our way through the crowd of officials blocking the entrance to the players' tunnel and up the sloping walkway which led back to the dressing-rooms.

We had to run the gauntlet of television cameras and microphones but we pushed our way through and burst into the dressing-room yelling our heads off. It was amazing.

Champagne corks popped and there were a few tears as we finally began to realize what we had done.

The backroom staff came in to have a drink with us and the Blackburn lads joined in too and were quick to offer their congratulations. But I knew exactly how they felt.

I wondered if they realized what a big favour we were doing them. Two years earlier when we had played Arsenal at the end of the 1991 season The Gunners had won the championship before that game started. They paraded their trophy and responded to the cheers of the crowd. We felt like gatecrashers at a party; now Blackburn were doing the same.

All they wanted to do was get changed and head out of Old Trafford as quickly as they could, but I bet that Kenny Dalglish wanted them to take notice of what was going on around them.

It's funny but the gaffer reckons that we all learned something at Highbury on the night they took the title and when you think about Blackburn's performance last season perhaps our big night had a similar effect on them.

Watching those Arsenal players celebrating and seeing how their supporters reacted to the success gave us a new hunger. It was something you had to be part of to fully understand what I mean. During the build-up to a big game coaches and managers often build up the excitement with stories of their own experiences, but until you see it for yourself words mean nothing. You find yourself going to what should be a normal League game then suddenly feeling that you are in the losers' dressing-room at a cup final. It was as bad as that.

Even if Blackburn had won it would have been a hollow victory, meaningless because we had already taken the honours. I suppose they could have claimed to be the first side to beat the champions, but we were having none of that. The result for them became just another statistic.

Our lads may not have realized it but the more we enjoyed ourselves, the more we were doing Kenny's job for him! He knew the feeling all right . He had reached the top many times with Liverpool, it was nothing new to him. Now he was getting an important message across to his players without having to say a word.

All he needed to do was open their dressing-room door and say, 'Do you want to have some of that next season?'

If Highbury was our turning-point in 1991, I bet I'm not far off the mark when I say that our big night at Old Trafford had a lot to do with Blackburn's attitude last season. No footballer likes to be an also-ran.

Kenny knew that if his players had anything about them they would respond to what they had seen. The same went for us of course. We had done it once. Would it be even better the second time around?

Taking the title was important to many people, not just Alex Ferguson and his players. For the older fans it meant their twenty-six years of patience was being rewarded; for the youngsters it was a new experience to see the championship pennant flying at Old Trafford.

As for our chairman, Martin Edwards, it was the result of years of hard work. He had striven to get United to the top with much of his effort going unnoticed by those who are quick to criticize. He was the man largely responsible for most of what was going on that night after carrying on where his late father left off.

Louis Edwards had spoken of his vision of creating an Old Trafford stadium which would be envied throughout the game. He wanted it to be a showpiece with more to offer football supporters than just a place to stand and watch their favourites. He gave his support to the various managers who followed Sir Matt in their efforts to bring success on the field. He helped to create a club with a strong financial backbone and began the building work which was coming to a conclusion even as we took the title.

His dream became reality but the sad thing was that he was not there to see his wish fulfilled.

During our barren years Martin took a hell of a lot of stick and I think it must have been a great thrill for him and the other directors when they saw the club back at the top.

From my own point of view the feeling was also one of relief. At last I was part of a championship-winning side after coming close so many times. I had begun to wonder if it would ever happen.

My first near miss was 17 years earlier when I was with West Brom. We had been challenging during the first few weeks of the season and by Christmas the bookies fancied us to do well. We had a great belief in our chances but it soon became apparent that we didn't really have enough depth in our squad. We began to pick up injuries and fell away finally finishing 3rd. That was a total choker and the memory has haunted me ever since.

Seventeen years is a long time for anyone to look back. For a footballer it is a lifetime, some players are not even in the game for that long. Seventeen years of coming close. Seventeen years of telling yourself perhaps you are not quite good enough.

I found myself involved in sides which have finished in the top 4 at least 14 times, so the expression 'so near and yet so far' has a familiar ring to me.

When you come close to success and are not quite able to grasp it, I suppose you can be forgiven for thinking that perhaps it might never come your way – 'Whatever will be will be,' as the Stretford Enders used to sing.

There are players who go through their career without winning any of the major prizes, and yet there are others who seem to have the Midas touch.

Look at Liverpool in their glory years. Those players were so used to winning the title they must have thought that you got championship medals for Christmas.

But do you realize that George Best never got to play in an FA Cup Final? That must have haunted him the way that missing out on the championship haunted me.

Some folk might be satisfied with what I had achieved but I wanted that little bit more. There was always that nagging wish to be part of a championship-winning side, and when I joined United that was my main aim and it was quickly made obvious to me that I was not alone. Everyone at the club had the same ambition.

So my feeling of satisfaction was immense as I looked around that packed dressing-room and listened to toast after toast: 'We've waited a long time for this. Here's to the champions!'

Denis Law, George Best and Bobby Charlton had all watched the game and it must have brought back some pleasant memories for them as well as for Sir Matt.

It was so fitting that Sir Matt was able to come and see us in the dressing-room. He stood there shaking hands with players who had only heard stories about the great achievements of his teams. Some were not even born the last time United had been champions.

Everyone knew Sir Matt of course because we saw him so often. He was at the club virtually every day. He would come in and sit in his office saying 'Hello son,' to every player who walked past the door, or stroll around the ground puffing on his pipe chatting to anyone and everyone who came up to speak to him.

I have a lasting memory of him chuckling his way from one end of the dressing-room to the other, savouring the moment. No-one realized it would be the last time he would join in such celebrations.

Sir Matt stood there smiling and posing for photographs. I think he had a picture taken with every single player. Here was a man who had seen it all before, calmly looking on as all around him there was total chaos.

The lads were in high spirits. We sprayed one another with champagne, shouting, yelling and laughing. Sir Matt said very little but his expression said everything. His beloved Manchester United were back at the top.

The celebrations continued well into the night and beyond. Most of the players went on a 3-week binge and I wondered if we would ever come back to earth.

It was such a contrast to the previous summer.

Twelve months earlier we had thrown it all away and had been so sickened when Leeds stole the championship from under our noses. Nobody would let us forget it. The disappointment was immense and we all wished we could hide away until the new season started.

That was impossible. Everywhere we went rival supporters taunted us. They did not seem too bothered that their own team had won nothing, they were just glad we had missed out. It is an attitude I cannot understand. If Leeds fans wanted to gloat, OK, but Manchester City?

Even the United faithful demanded an explanation about what went wrong. We had no real answer. We had tried, but just when it looked as if we would cruise to the title it slipped away. We were devastated.

They all had their theories. Too many changes, too many games in the final run-in, pure bad luck. We tried our best and it was not good enough, and the gloaters gloated.

I remember when we had played Liverpool at the end of the 1991–92 season on the day Leeds beat Sheffield United. The result left us with no alternative – we had to win to stay in the chase. We lost. Some Liverpool fans had a banner which read: 'Have you ever seen United win the League?'

Being able to put things right by the following summer made it doubly satisfying. Those words were a thing of the past.

There was no reason for us to say anything. Our success said it all. Football's failures of one season were the champions of the next. Say no more.

Steve and I had collected the trophy together so we decided we might as well do the same when it came to holidays. Denise is friendly with Steve's wife Janet, so a fortnight after the season ended we packed up and flew out to Portugal. We had a great time.

That feeling of achievement was still there. A deep satisfaction as we lay on the beach and the kids played together in the sand. We could have a few drinks knowing that nobody would come up to us and have a go. No-one was going to ask that question I had heard so many times before: 'When are you going to win the title?'

The fans did approach us – that is nothing new – but the majority were United supporters who just wanted an autograph, to shake hands, or offer us a drink. We could have spent the whole holiday freeloading and legless. What surprised us was the way the knockers disappeared when they had nothing to knock!

However, all good things have to come to an end and soon

the holiday was over and it was back to Manchester. When we got home it soon became obvious that our success was having a tremendous effect on everybody who followed United. Old Trafford looked as if it had been turned into a theme park. Coachloads of fans rolled up to have a look at the championship trophy, tour the stadium and buy souvenirs. If we went anywhere near the ground we were surrounded by fans.

It was a similar story at The Cliff, the club's training ground in Salford. By the time the summer break was over and we checked in for pre-season training the school holidays were in full flow. We found ourselves under siege.

There has always been a big following for United but it seemed to have doubled in a matter of weeks. We were supposed to be preparing for the new season but half the time was spent signing autographs. Jim McGregor, the physio, reckoned the biggest threat to fitness was going to be writer's cramp!

Training began. Run, run, run.

The talk in and out of the dressing-room seemed to be about the same subject.

The tabloids had pointed out that since our FA Cup win in 1990 we had gradually been rolling into a fairly formidable outfit. The European Cup-Winners' Cup, the Coca-Cola Cup, more wins in two seasons than anyone else.

Were the champions capable of holding on to that title?

Well, could we?

That was certainly going to be our aim, to be the first United side since the famous Busby Babes to top the table two years in succession. The Babes did it in 1956 and 1957, we were ready to set our eyes on 1994.

It also made us realize how short-lived success is. We knew we could all get out the videos of the previous season and enjoy those great wins against Sheffield Wednesday, Crystal Palace and Norwich, but it was history.

The championship dust had hardly settled, yet the fans in the car park at The Cliff were asking us, 'Can you do it again this season?'

As for the sports pages the experts all said that we were going to do well in Europe . . . but enough said about that for the moment.

You always need a target in life and even though winning the championship had taken a millstone from around our necks, the feeling amongst the players was that we all wanted to leave our own mark. We felt that we wanted to do something no other United side had ever done.

It was during the first week of pre-season training that one of the lads mentioned the double. Usually that would mean that he had a couple of certs for the afternoon's big race meeting but this time we all knew what he meant.

The League and the FA Cup, now that would be something.

It was nothing more than dressing-room chat, one of those general conversations we have before or after a training session, but we knew that we had to be in with a shout. You only had to look at our performances over the two previous seasons to see that it would take a serious drop in form for us not to be challenging for one of the honours. Why not more than one?

I had a bit more on my mind. While we had been on holiday I had had time to think about the future. Was I about to start my last season as a player? If so what was next?

I was uncertain what was going to happen but at least I had been saved from making an early decision when the club offered me an extension to my contract. The gaffer asked me to sign for another year and I was quite happy to do so because I still felt that I had something to offer as a player.

I had been tossing things over in my mind and worked out that my main rivals for my position in central midfield were Brian McClair, Mickey Phelan, Clayton Blackmore, Darren Ferguson and Nicky Butt.

Brian is a striker and a good one at that, but because of the arrival of Eric Cantona he has found himself moved back into midfield by the manager. It's a role he's filled reluctantly at times but he's the sort of player who'd play in goal if they asked him.

Mickey is a real workhorse who has been in the game for a long time but he's found himself struggling to keep a regular place in the first team.

As for Clayton he has been unlucky to be hit by so many injuries at the wrong time. Two hernia operations kept him out for most of last season but he still managed to win back his place in the Welsh national side.

In Darren, the manager's son, I saw a real contender. He was doing well in the Reserves. He was second team skipper and it had to be harder for him because, although nobody ever regarded him as Alex's son, he must have felt that he had to give that bit more because he was. Surely my experience would count?

Young Nicky is definitely one for the future. He plays my kind of game and there are sure signs that he will make it. But could he keep me out of the side at the start of the new season? I thought not.

So when I signed my new contract I felt that I could hold off the challengers.

Then came a shock.

While we were on holiday the papers had been full of speculation that United were about to plunge for a new player. He had been linked with the club for months, but this was nothing new. If the boss had signed everyone whose name had been associated with United since he arrived he would have a squad of 400 and the club would be bankrupt!

This time it turned out to be true. He bought Roy Keane from Nottingham Forest in a record deal of close on £4 million.

I suppose I was prepared for it, but then the truth began to dawn. United had bought the player who was going to replace me. I was ready to face the challenge from the others in the squad but you don't spend that sort of money on a substitute.

Roy arrived and the situation became all too clear to me. It was a strange feeling but it must have been the same when I was bought by United and Sammy McIlroy realized he was being replaced.

Sammy moved on. I was staying. I was determined to show everybody that I was far from finished.

By mid July I was getting back to full fitness when we came to an important part of the pre-season build-up. We flew out to South Africa for a two match visit to play in a friendly tournament against Arsenal, who had won both the FA Cup and the League Cup, and Kaiser Chiefs, the top team in that part of the world.

It was 20 July; I had 19 days to prove to the manager that I was good enough to play against Arsenal again, this time in the Charity Shield at Wembley.

The players who had been on international duty with England were left behind to have the break they had missed because they had gone to America. The rest of us got ready for 10 days in the African sun and some tough training sessions. With the regulars missing, those on the fringe of the squad were given an extra chance to catch the boss's eye. Although I didn't consider myself to be a fringe player I saw it as the perfect opportunity to prove to myself that I could still do it.

We did the usual build up to fitness, plenty of running and exercise. Then we got down to ball work. From a playing viewpoint everything was fine. I felt fit and I had no problems. But the trip turned into a total nightmare for me.

Five days in, we played Arsenal in Johannesburg's Ellis Stadium, a rugby union ground that's about 6,000 feet above sea level. Forget the altitude, I felt like digging a big hole and jumping in it. For the first time in my career I called a referee a cheat. He sent me off.

It may have seemed nothing, although it made a few head-lines back home, but the repercussions hit me like a sledgehammer some weeks later. The dismissal, in a pre-season friendly, was to lead to a suspension which would put me out of the side at a crucial stage of the new season.

Conditions in the stadium were far from perfect. It was very hot and dusty and there was a huge crowd. We felt that the referee was favouring Arsenal with his decisions, but this was probably because the crowd seemed to be on our side. He gave them a dubious penalty and they scored. Then we had what looked like two genuine penalty claims rejected and my temperature went up.

I have been in the game long enough to know that they were worth a shout. Most experienced referees would have given us a spot kick for one if not both of our claims. Not him . . .

But he did give another to Arsenal. Two nil!

I was furious and lost my temper. I know that I should have shown a bit more self-control but I had seen enough. That referee had pushed me over the edge.

The first words that came into my head were: 'Referee. You're a cheat!'

His reply was also straight to the point: 'You're off!'

Out came the red card, and after giving him a stare that let him know exactly how I felt, I walked.

Who was he? Some referee unknown as far as we were concerned, not one of the FIFA regulars we meet on the circuit. It turned out that he was an Irish rugby union ref. who had gone to live in South Africa.

He certainly made the most of his big moment. In my entire career I had only been sent off just once before. As I walked from the field I was furious.

I kept telling myself that it was nothing more than an exhibition game but that bloke was taking things very seriously indeed. The Arsenal players sympathized but there was no way back.

I think that a more experienced soccer official might have handled things differently, but no. I was told there was a chance I would miss a couple of league games when we got back home. The referee would argue that he was only doing his job but he was also going to stop me from doing mine. I just cannot agree that bookings or sendings off in friendly games, or pre-season tournaments outside England, should affect anyone's appearances in serious league or cup games. The goals are never added to a player's record, the results are meaningless, why should disciplinary action count?

I suppose there is a fear that such games could get out of hand if there is no form of punishment, that a player might deliberately try to injure an opponent knowing he could get away with it, but then officials could make exceptions. No-one was going to get hurt by a few words said in the heat of the moment.

I accept that I have always been the type of player whose approach to the game can lead to bookings. I am aggressive, I like making strong challenges, and if they go wrong then I am ready to face the consequences.

For most of my career I have been given the responsibility of skippering teams, and because of this have been regarded as the spokesman on the field. The knockers have accused me of trying to influence officials, or whingeing at decisions, but they don't know what's being said. They don't know that most professional footballers have a good relationship with the officials. What can look like a disputed decision may be nothing more than a hurried 'What's that for?'

The majority of first-class referees give you an answer which is all you are asking. You might not agree, but you have to accept it and get on with the game.

In professional football there is a lot at stake and refereeing decisions can change results. So as someone who likes to get involved, my disciplinary record has not been too bad. I could certainly have done without that South African stain on my character.

The only other time I was sent off was at Roker Park, where I have never been flavour of the month since the Sunderland fans found out that I supported Newcastle when I was a boy. In that game I was booed every time I touched the ball and I'm sure that sort of thing must influence things slightly. One slip and the crowd is on your back.

What happened was that a linesman reckoned I had deliberately kicked Barry Venison on the side of the head. The referee never saw the incident but I think the linesman only saw half of what happened too. Barry and I finished up on the ground after a challenge and he was holding me back as I tried to get to the loose ball. As I stepped over him my trailing foot caught his head. There was nothing malicious, it was just one of those things that can happen during a game.

The crowd reacted. It probably seemed to those 50 yards away that Barry had been pole-axed by a vicious attack! I was sent off, Barry carried on playing. I accepted my punishment but I know in my heart of hearts that I did not deliberately kick him.

In my defence I would simply say this. Do you think that if a professional footballer intentionally kicked someone on the head, they would be fit enough to continue?

So our visit to South Africa left a lasting impression for the wrong reasons, as far as I was concerned. It was a shame that my one moment of frustration spoiled everything.

Before the game we had spent a few days looking round the Province. I had been before but that had been a fairly sheltered visit. This time we went right into the heart of the townships and saw the contrast between our way of life back home and the white suburbs of Johannesburg. I remember the drive from the airport to our hotel on the morning we arrived. We saw big houses just like those on the Cheshire side of Manchester where many of us live, but these were different. Many of them had high walls round them and some went as far as electrified fencing and barbed wire.

We went to Zambesi township just outside Johannesburg where

there is a squatter camp and saw families living in huts made from old pieces of wood and sheets of corrugated steel. They were just ordinary folk being forced to live in terrible conditions and hopefully we brought a little light into their lives.

They came out in their hundreds to see us. Manchester United is a name that is known everywhere. Football is an international language.

We met the local kids and had a kick about with them, signed autographs and handed out souvenirs. I suppose that is one thing I will always owe to football. The game has been my life and it has taken me to some amazing places over the years. It is a debt I will find it impossible to repay.

I often tell young players who are just starting off that there is a great big world waiting for them out there. We come from ordinary backgrounds and if we are successful we get to places beyond the dreams of most people.

Travelling can be an education. Not in the geographical sense – although there have been times when we have got the maps out to see just where we are – but in life itself.

The experience of visiting different countries makes you aware of the contrasting cultures and how lucky we are. All of us were fully aware of the problems in South Africa, especially as the country was getting closer to its first democratic elections when black people would have as much right to vote as the whites. Despite what some folk think, footballers read the front-page stories in the newspapers as well as the back.We also spend an above average-time watching television news reports especially during those away trips when we find ourselves stuck in an hotel bedroom with little else to do.

We went to South Africa open-minded and prepared for any-thing. There is a chance that we could have been taken to selected areas, but if that is the case then nobody prevented us from doing just what we wanted. It seemed that the breakdown of apartheid was working but more recent events have shown that there is still a long way to go. We have all paid special interest to the happenings over there since our visit.

We went to Soweto, a place which makes the news for all the wrong reasons. There were a few raised eyebrows amongst the lads when we discovered we were due to go there, and we were surprised to find out that the area has more than one football stadium. We imagined it to be a place where nothing went on but trouble.

We went to take a coaching session in the old Orlando Pirates ground with the kids from the South African FA Coaching Scheme. They were amazing. They were so enthusiastic for football it was great to see. It could have been that because there is little else for them to do they have turned their energy to soccer, but they live for the game. Whatever the reason, it is football, football and more football.

Unlike the kids back home they can't go off to their room to watch television or play computer games. They have none of the luxuries our kids take for granted.

In a way I suppose it was just like that when I was at school. All me and my pals wanted to do was get a ball out, form a couple of teams and play against each other till we all got a sharp reminder from somebody's parents that it was dark, we had missed our tea . . . and as for homework . . . ? That, as they say, is another story!

The young Africans also showed us something that seems to be missing amongst many of the kids we meet at home nowadays. Discipline. They would stand around in an orderly fashion and listen to every word we had to say. If you were demonstrating a skill they would watch every movement, wait until you gave the signal, then practise it with amazing dedication.

The discipline could have had something to do with their coaches being strict, but I didn't see any signs that the kids were frightened. Surely that would have come across if they felt threatened.

No, it probably comes down to a lesson in life most of us were taught as youngsters but so many have quickly forgotten – simply doing what they were told.

Those kids loved being with us and the feeling was mutual. They had the time of their lives and I think I can say that the same goes for every member of the United squad. Here were children being raised in one of the most violent atmospheres imaginable, some of them living in conditions close to squalor, and yet all they wanted to do was kick a football and learn as much as they could about the game.

As for the threat of violence, we never felt in any danger nor did we experience any hostility towards us and we went into the townships without a police escort. We did have some minders but they were there to keep the overenthusiastic autograph hunters at bay rather than protect us from any threats.

I would have liked to have seen even more of the country but it was not possible on such a short tour, and as usual we spent a lot of our time relaxing at the hotel after training. Those trips into the outlying districts and the evening sessions we spent talking to massed groups of United supporters were a break in the routine.

I am sure that the people of the townships respected the club for taking the trouble to go and see them. They saw it as a gesture made on behalf of sport, and it was clear to us that we were very welcome. It was as if they looked up to us, as if they appreciated that we were making an effort to go and see them. They regarded us as something special, British footballers from a club as famous as Manchester United in their township to see them and help to teach their kids about the game. All we were giving was some of our time, but they regarded it as something special. I would like to have done more.

There had been talk back home that it was a risk, that some fanatics might use the visit as a way of publicizing their cause, but I have felt in more danger riding on the team coach to a normal Saturday away game than I did over there!

Before our fixture against Kaiser Chiefs we were introduced to Nelson Mandela and I was surprised to discover that he knew the names of all our players. He also managed to get himself onto the team photograph and that made it one for the souvenir album. We all reckon that he's a United fan!

We drew 0–0 with the Chiefs and this time I managed to stay on the field. The next day we said our farewells with many of the lads promising to return for a holiday. Then it was home to Manchester – and quickly down to earth.

After a 14-hour flight we went straight from the airport to The Cliff for a training session. We had a game the next day.

We had to get ready for a friendly against Benfica at Old Trafford, a match that was part of the celebrations organized to mark the twenty-fifth anniversary of the club's European Cup win. Once again it made us realize the importance of winning that championship. For the first time since 1969, when the club had qualified as holders, we were in the European Champions Cup.

No-one was too bothered that Benfica beat us 1–0. The result was unimportant when you took into account the travelling we had done in the previous 48 hours. From a personal point of view I felt I had given one of the best performances during any of the build-up games.

As for Roy Keane, he had not played particularly well during the tour. It was nothing for him to worry about, he was still adjusting to being with a new club.

It is something I experienced myself. When I came to Old Trafford, United paid West Brom £1.5 million, which was a record at the time. It took me a while to settle in. No matter how hard you try, you can't stop thinking about the fee. How can a club have spent so much money on you?

You feel the burden of responsibility no matter how many times the manager tells you there is nothing to worry about. Those thoughts haunt you and you start to ask yourself all sorts of questions. Will you be a success? Can you live up to your reputation? Will the others accept you?

Roy had risen from the obscurity of Irish football to join Forest for £20,000. Before signing for us he discovered he was a wanted man. He had offers from Blackburn and Arsenal and that would make him realize that he was moving into the big league. But from £20,000 to £4 million is a massive step.

Coming to Manchester United was also different from anything he would have experienced before and he had to learn to handle the new set-up. It is the biggest club in the country and it can be difficult for a player to settle, even though there are no obvious pressures from within. Like it or not you are always in the spotlight. There are constant media demands for interviews, television appearances and photographs. Some can thrive on it, others find it pressurizing.

On top of that you have to get to know your new colleagues just like any other job, and I think Roy really needed that settling-in period. Going to South Africa must have been invaluable.

Players regard pre-season tours as a break from the daily routine of getting back to full fitness. Using the trip to weigh up his new team-mates must have been a big help to Roy.

Since then he has showed that he was a shrewd buy and I have had to accept that when Roy and Paul Ince are on top form they would make it very difficult for anyone to get a place in the side. They work well together, but I would like to feel that when I played alongside Incey we were also a sound midfield.

When Paul first joined United there were those who said that I was having an adverse effect on his game. They claimed his best performances were when I was out of the side and perhaps he felt overawed playing alongside me. What a load of rubbish.

In the period immediately after his controversial transfer from West Ham, Paul was still a young player learning the game. Part of his education was to adapt to United's approach. By the time it came to the championship season Incey had matured not only on the field but off it as well. The fact that he seemed to be playing better without me was more to do with his maturing than any influence I was supposed to have had on him.

He had also settled in the Manchester area and he and his wife had a baby son. Players change when they have families. When young Tom Ince came along Paul realized that he now had responsibilities and he grew up as a man as well as a player. Gone was the Jack the Lad from the East End. He transformed into a top-class international footballer as well as a dedicated family man. He always had the talent, now he had the purpose in life to use it.

I have seen it happen before. Players mature somewhere between 24 and 26 years of age and the change can be quite dramatic. They turn from kids into men. Paul was no different to anyone else.

Don't get me wrong, there is still a fun side to 'The Guv'nor' and you keep well out of the way when he and his mate Ryan Giggs start messing about after training – especially if there is a hosepipe handy and you are relaxing in the bath!

As for Roy, he seemed a quiet lad when he arrived – most players are. They take it coolly at first, no-one wants to breeze in as if they have been there for years. He wanted to find his feet but he mixed in well and made new friends. It had to be quite an experience for him being bought for a record fee by the club that had just won the championship.

I remember my thoughts when I moved to Old Trafford, wondering about being accepted in the dressing-room and whether there would be any wisecracks about the big fee. But it is not like that at United.

Anyone starting a new job will worry, that is only natural. One thing a new player does escape these days is the leg-pulling and the practical jokes.

When I arrived it was in the reign of Lou Macari, the king of them all. Anything could happen when he was around and it didn't matter if you were the longest-serving player or the new boy. It wasn't unusual to find your shoes nailed to the floor, or the toes cut out of your socks, but strangely when Louie left it all stopped!

I was also luckier than Roy when I signed because I had a few friends already at the club. Ray Wilkins, Steve Coppell and Gary Bailey were all in the England squad with me, and I was bought by Ron Atkinson who had been my manager at West Brom for the previous four years.

As far as I know the only player Roy was already friendly with was Denis Irwin, his Republic of Ireland team-mate, but he made up for that pretty quickly.

Settling in is just one of the things that can affect a player's performance. New training routines, a slightly different role on the field or even the pressures of house-hunting have got to some.

It took Gary Pallister quite a while to adapt to playing for a big club after his move from Middlesbrough but he came through well.

As long as a player is strong-minded enough then it will work out for him, and Roy Keane is certainly that. He knows where he wants to go and he will get there.

Despite the challenge from Roy I was feeling in good condition as the start of the season got closer. We both began the game against Benfica, with Paul missing following the England tour to America. I played 86 minutes before being substituted and was feeling fine.

Training continued and three days later we had our last pre-season friendly before the Charity Shield. Wembley was my target, I wanted to be in the side for that one, and when the boss named the line-up for the game against Celtic at Old Trafford I felt that I stood a good chance.

I started in midfield alongside Incey. Roy was on the bench. It was supposed to be a friendly but both sets of players took it seriously and you could tell that Celtic wanted to win. What a great boost that would have been for their manager Liam Brady who was under quite a bit of pressure. If they could have beaten the English champions he could have gone back to Glasgow ready for anything the new season might bring.

No chance. We took it 1–0 thanks to an Andrei Kanchelskis goal. It was a commentator's nightmare, that one, a Kanchelskis shot deflected past Pat Bonner by Dariusz Wdowczyk!

At half-time the gaffer made a switch. He was looking for fresh legs and took me off to make way for Roy. I was quietly confident though. I wasn't being pulled out because I was playing badly, he just wanted to try out another option in midfield.

I watched the rest of the game, reflecting on my build-up. Training had gone well, the pre-season performances had been satisfactory and I was looking forward to the weekend when we would face Arsenal for the first time since that Johannesburg fiasco. This time it was at Wembley in the traditional curtain-raiser to the season.

It was the first time United had played in the game as champions since 1968 and this would be a new experience for all of us. We had been there before as cup-winners but this time there would be something special about the occasion.

But then came a blow. I was dropped. My first disappointment of the season, before it had even started.

The gaffer reckoned that he needed another look at Roy and Paul playing together before the serious stuff started. They had played only half a game. So I was left out.

I could understand the thinking behind it, but it was still hard to take. I felt I had played as well as anybody in the pre-season games and expected that to count.

But the manager had paid nearly £4 million for Roy, and Incey was playing really well, carrying on where he had left off during the championship season. I knew I would have to stand down.

It's a funny thing, but no matter how many years you have been playing you still want to be in the side when the season kicks off.

It was a weird feeling going to Wembley for a big game – and no matter what the critics might say the Charity Shield is a big event – knowing I was fully fit, yet not being out there at the start. The frustration I felt as I sat there on the bench was immense and I couldn't get on quick enough when the manager changed things round in the 68th minute.

Mark Hughes and Ian Wright scored and it ended 1-1.

However, the 1993 game was different. The FA had decided that there would be a winner and, instead of each club holding the shield for six months as they had done in the past, there was a penalty shoot-out.

Now, it isn't my favourite way of settling issues and we have had our fair share of bad luck in similar situations in recent years. Twice I have seen us knocked out of European competitions, and we were the first ever First Division club to go out of the FA Cup on spot kicks when the new rule was introduced, losing to Southampton at Old Trafford in 1992.

Not this time though. We won the shoot-out and I managed to convert my penalty. It was ironic really: there we were playing Arsenal again and this time there were no arguments about penalties!

The season had yet to start and we had our first piece of silverware. We felt it would not be the last. We were ready for whatever lay ahead.

The Charity Shield is only a friendly and players know this. Nobody goes totally flat out. With the season just a week away they don't fly into tackles as they would in a cup final, but they still want to win. Nobody likes losing at Wembley.

Next day when we reported for training at The Cliff, I went in for a chat with the manager and told him that I felt that I should have been playing in the game right from the start. The boss is approachable in these situations and will always listen to what a player has to say. He seemed to appreciate my views and I could well have influenced his thoughts.

When he named his side for the opening game at Norwich I was playing!

CHAPTER TWO
Double Vision

ERIC CANTONA WAS THE ONLY ONE OF OUR SQUAD WHO COULD really claim to have 'been there, done that' as the opening day of the new season arrived. He began the 1992–93 campaign with Leeds when they had set out to defend their title. Now it was our turn. For the majority of the lads it was a totally fresh experience and I was not the only one who was looking forward to it.

I have to admit that even after all my years in the game I got quite a thrill as I flicked through the match programme for our first game at Norwich and saw the words of their chairman Robert Chase: 'Welcome to Manchester United, the league champions.' There it was in black and white, the message I had always wanted to read.

The same greeting would be extended to us throughout the season, but I am sure that the programme editors would have loved to have added a few more words of truth '. . . the side everybody wants to beat!' What better scalp to take than that of the champions?

We were going to be up against it. Once you are at the top of the mountain you have two options – stay there or come down. We had no intention of descending for a long time but there would be plenty of teams trying to push us over the edge.

Opponents have always raised their game against Manchester United and we take that as a compliment. However, some of the tactics used against us, and the pressures from the media we were to face in the months ahead, made it clear that it is tough at the top. It seems that there is a British tradition of putting people on a pedestal, then knocking them off. Even before we had kicked a ball the knives were out.

Manchester United stories sell newspapers and we are all aware of that, but some of the things which appear in print go way over the top. The bigger you are the harder they try to hit you, and the old adage of 'print and be damned' has these days been replaced with the slogan 'don't let the truth spoil a good story'!

One example was a big spread of pictures of Ryan Giggs enjoying himself on holiday. Nothing wrong with that but the headline read something like: 'Birds, booze and boobs!' implying that Giggsy had gone on a massive binge as soon as the boss's back was turned. He was actually sipping a drink on a beach with a group of friends who happened to include some pretty girls wearing bikini bottoms. It was a typical modern summer scene.

The implication was that he was on some sort of drunken romp which might threaten his career and understandably the boss went into a fury. The paper had sent a photographer and reporter to track down Ryan while he was on holiday and stir things up. It was not one of the regular football writers who did the article but a news reporter who might never come into contact with Fergie. If I was him I would make sure I never did!

They call it 'hit and run', the tactics used time and again for muck-raking, and it led to a red card for the local man. He carried the can and for a while was banned from the manager's press conferences even though he personally was innocent.

It was a typical example of what happens these days. Giggsy had been given the royal treatment, which has nothing to do with red carpets and bouquets. The long-lens brigade picked him out hoping his top would slip off!

We have all had to learn to put up with that sort of thing since the newspapers' approach to football reporting changed. Once upon a time a reporter went to a game and wrote about what he saw. It still happens in the quality papers, but the tabloids go for the sensational. Their stories centre around quotes picked up from a manager or players. The more controversial the quote the bigger splash it gets.

As our new season was about to kick-off we knew another tradition had also gone. For as long as most of us can remember football has been played at three o'clock on a Saturday afternoon. The first day of the season is when all clubs start equal. Each has the same number of points, nobody has won, drawn or lost more than anyone else.

Unfortunately the intervention of television has put paid to that and I don't regard it as a change for the better. Nowadays the season starts on a Saturday for the majority, on a Sunday for some, then by the Monday night the ones who get the short straw can find themselves playing their second game.

The Football Association announced the new fixture list during the summer and we discovered that we were to be the Sunday spectacular. We had a longer wait than the others and that was why we found ourselves ourselves sitting around the breakfast table in the team hotel in Norwich instead of having a day at home with our families. But those managers' quotes from the Saturday games made interesting reading!

The main topic of conversation was what had gone on the previous day. 'Arsenal 0 Coventry City 3; Aston Villa 4 Queen's Park Rangers 1 . . .' I read through the results as Steve Bruce and Gary Pallister ordered more tea and toast.

There were certainly some surprises. Blackburn had done well, beating Chelsea 2–1 at Stamford Bridge, Liverpool had won their home game against Sheffield Wednesday 2–0, but Newcastle had gone down 1–0 to Tottenham at St James's Park in their first game back in the top section. That was an upset. I had fancied them to get off to a good start. Their passionate home support has always given them an advantage.

That Arsenal scoreline certainly got the lads talking. We all had our opinions about who might pose the biggest challenge during the new season and Arsenal were high on everyone's list, but to be honest, Coventry were not amongst the fancied runners!

Arsenal were there because of their experience, and we also felt that the teams which had run us close the previous season would be involved once again. I know Aston Villa finished 10 points behind us but they did beat us twice on their ground in the league and the Coca-Cola Cup. Norwich had also been involved and we would find out later that day if they had improved.

Blackburn were seen as a definite threat. Jack Walker, their chairman, is what they mean by a benefactor. He is ready to spend his millions on anybody Kenny Dalglish fancies, and Kenny has a pretty shrewd idea of what he's looking for. Alan Shearer had recovered from injury and when they added David Batty early in the new season it completed the Dalglish jigsaw. We expected them to push us and they did.

And what about ourselves? We had the squad and the confidence and we would soon find out if the hunger was still there. We wanted to carry on where we had left off. We knew that Leeds had slumped in the season following their title win but felt sure our chances were better because of the depth of our squad.

There had been a few digs in that week's papers that we might not be up to it. There were predictions that Eric Cantona would not be with us by the end of the season and that the distraction of Europe was going to affect our form in the league. Rubbish!

And what about the evidence gleaned from the first afternoon of the new season? Of the ten Premiership games played, six had ended in away wins. Six. Could we make it seven?

Ipswich had beaten Oldham 3–0 at Boundary Park, Everton won 2–0 at Southampton and Wimbledon by the same scoreline at West Ham. Only Villa, Liverpool and Sheffield United (who beat Swindon 3–1), had won on their own grounds, with the one draw being at Maine Road where City and Leeds finished 1–1.

Just as one swallow doesn't make a summer, one day's results can hardly be a reflection of what to expect for the rest of the season, but reading through those Sunday reports you would have thought that it was all over. They obviously get the London editions in Norwich and the papers were full of stories about the demise of the Gunners and how Tottenham looked set to sweep to glory after beating Newcastle. Little did they know . . .

As for our game, the tipsters seemed to be evenly balanced. Some fancied Norwich, some us, but the majority took the easy option of a draw.

It makes entertaining Sunday morning reading but nobody really knows what is going to happen in a game. Matches can go according to form but a bounce of the ball, a dodgy decision by the referee, an offside flag that stays down, can change the outcome. That is the fascination of football, yet we all try to predict results.

Hope comes into it. Ask a supporter what they think a result might be and they will tell you what they *hope* will happen. Hope is what we all have at the start of a new season. All I hoped was that I was playing!

Even though the boss had told me at the beginning of the week that I was in the side, I had a sneaking feeling that I might just be edged out at the last minute. Eric Cantona was injured and I thought that Brian McClair might get the vote ahead of me. He could have played up front with Sparky, but when the boss named the team I was there. He said it was on the strength of my pre-season performances.

Alex decided to field a 4–5–1 formation with Paul Parker, Steve Bruce, Gary Pallister and Denis Irwin across the back and Mark Hughes up front on his own. I was in a fairly full midfield along with Roy Keane and Paul Ince. Ryan Giggs and Andrei Kanchelskis were on the flanks. Lee Sharpe, Brian McClair and Les Sealey occupied the seats on the bench, with Les playing his dual role of back up 'keeper to Peter Schmeichel and unofficial cheerleader!

What a guy he is. They say that goalkeepers are barmy and Les fits that description perfectly, but he is also a dedicated professional who works hard yet is always ready for a laugh. The United fans loved him and it was a sad time when he was freed in the summer of 1994.

That was a long way off as we ran out at Carrow Road to a rousing welcome from our travelling supporters. They filled one section of the grandstand opposite the players' tunnel. I think they got as big a kick out of chanting 'We are the champions' as we did listening to them.

So we were on our way.

We expected a tough battle because Norwich would be smarting after the run-around we had given them the previous season but they played defensively. At no time did we feel in any danger but I have got to say I was surprised by Mike Walker's tactics.

The Norwich manager had obviously been haunted by what had happened the last time we had been to Carrow Road, when the speed of Giggsy and Andrei had cut them to ribbons. He was taking no chances this time and played with a sweeper in an effort to stifle our quick breaks.

The gaffer kept things quiet about Eric's injury and his plan worked. I am certain Norwich thought he would be involved and felt they had worked out a scheme to keep him quiet. Alex has often been criticized by the media for giving duff team information, but he has a theory that the less the opposition know about your plans the better. It may sound trivial but why should you help your opponent work out a way of beating you?

There are times when it is going to be obvious what the team will be – if you have played the same line-up for six consecutive wins, for instance. But if a key player picks up an injury in training why shout about it? Cloak and dagger stuff? Not really, it goes on all the time and the media play their part. The local reporters who follow Norwich would have been in contact with their opposite numbers in Manchester to swap team news. Are you telling me that they would not have gone straight to Mike Walker if they found out Cantona was going to be missing?

So the smoke-screen worked and the sweeper system backfired. Our five in midfield were able to block out any threats and it gave us a lot of possession which caught them out.

Ryan Giggs got our first goal, just as he did when we had beaten them the previous May, and Norwich must have felt that the nightmare was happening all over again. Mark Hughes was very much at the hub of things: 25 minutes had gone when Sparky saw his chance and tried to chip Bryan Gunn. With the 'keeper off his line the ball struck the crossbar and rebounded to the edge of the penalty area where Ryan was running in. He hit a low hard drive and that was it.

Mark made the second. I scored it!

We had gone off at half time leading 1–0 and the boss told us to keep things going the way they were. We were holding the ball in midfield and making Norwich come at us. This meant they were leaving gaps at the back we could exploit. Ten minutes into the second half and my chance came.

We were on the edge of their box when the ball was played low to Sparky. It was a half chance but he turned it into a certainty thanks to his quick thinking. Once upon a time he would have gone for the spectacular, but nowadays that only happens if there are no other opportunities open to him. He has become the complete centre forward.

As a young player he always showed that he had the ability to make it to the top but there was something missing. His first touch was amazing, he could pluck the ball down from anywhere and control it immediately; but as soon as he was called upon to make a telling pass it would go wrong.

The time he spent with Barcelona changed all that and we have Terry Venables to thank for some of the transformation which turned him into one of the best there is. He will still score those sensational goals but he is also much more aware of those around him. He creates as many opportunities as he hits match-winners.

Add that to his battling abilities and you will see why so many fellow professionals admire Mark. He will fight for every ball and wrestle his way through against opponents who kick bits off him week after week.

At Carrow Road as the ball reached him he knew he could go at goal but some of the angles were covered. Instead he flicked a pass back between his legs and into my path. It was a peach of a ball and I smacked it home.

Two-nil! The best possible start with three points away from home against one of the previous season's top sides.

I had no aspirations of pushing for leading scorer but it was nice to be on level terms with young Ryan. Earlier that week a group of friends had asked who I felt might be our top scorer this time round and I told them I fancied Giggsy could be up there. Eric Cantona was clear favourite. He had only been with us for three-quarters of the previous season and his nine strikes included some vitally important goals.

Mark would also be involved, but I had a sneaking feeling it might by Ryan's year and it was no surprise when he scored our first goal of the season. His game is improving all the time and I was sure that we were about to see him reach another stage of his development. He is a player of immense talent but I think we have only seen the tip of the iceberg so far.

Like Mark Hughes, Ryan has to work on certain aspects of his game to turn him into a world-class player. But unlike Mark I don't see any necessity for him to go abroad to improve his game, even though the temptation at times must be immense.

We are constantly reading stories that AC Milan want him and figures like a £15 million transfer deal have been bandied about. Only Ryan knows what he has planned for the future, but he is such a straightforward, down to earth lad who loves his life in Manchester, I don't think it includes a spell abroad.

The one weakness of his game was similar to the area Sparky had to work on and showed through time and again during the 1992–93 season. Ryan would demonstrate some magnificent skills, sprinting past defenders and getting down to the bye-line, then his final cross would be hit too low and would be easily cleared. Or he would weave his way downfield and get into a one-to-one situation with the goalkeeper, then either miss the target or see his shot smothered. It is nothing that cannot be put right and it is all part of the learning process that every successful player has gone through. He knows he has to work at it and it will come right in the end.

I have seen Ryan the boy become a youth and the youth a young man, and I am certain that if he continues his progress he will be one of the top players in Europe . . . and hopefully with Manchester United! It could be 4 or 5 years before we see the final product but it will be well worth the wait. Players usually mature between 24 to 26 years of age and when Ryan reaches that period of his career he should be something special.

It is unfortunate that he has been compared with George Best, although I have to admit that there are similarities in certain aspects of both his game and his appearance. But what a tremendous compliment.

There can be no argument that George was probably the best player in the world when he was at his peak. In those days the argument was, 'Who is the best, George or Pele?' Any answer is irrelevant. Both were world-class players and there are many who see in Ryan some of that same talent George possessed. It must mean that he has the potential to become one hell of a player.

Besty had an amazing passing range, was a superb finisher and topped our scoring charts time after time. That is where Ryan's improvements need to be made. If he can work on making his passing more accurate and add that lethal touch to his finishing, he will become one of the best players in the world, if not *the* best.

With those first three points in the bag the journey back to Manchester seemed shorter, and we were already planning for the first home game which was coming up three days later. The opposition was Dave Bassett's Sheffield United, the side which somehow had managed to beat us twice in 1992–93. They pipped us in the opening Premier League game at Bramall Lane and later in the season knocked us out of the FA Cup on an afternoon best forgotten.

They probably did us a bit of a favour even though we did not realize it at the time. Being out of the cup competitions meant we were able to concentrate on the championship in the way that Leeds had done in 1992 when we knocked them out of both cups.

So early in the season nobody was thinking too seriously about the double, but we knew we definitely had the appetite for success and wanted to go one better than the previous campaign if possible. And no-one was hungrier than Roy Keane. He was on the sharp end of a few wisecracks when we discovered that the only medal he had won during his Forest days was for victory in the Zenith Data Systems Cup! Now he was helping us to defend our title and we were determined to add to his collection.

Eric was still injured but there was no secret about it this time as we faced the Blades unchanged. The gaffer rearranged the formation slightly to give us a 4–3–3 line-up and there was a buzz about the crowd before the kick-off. Roy could not have asked for a better start to his United career.

Dave Bassett's sides are always difficult to beat, especially when they set their stall out to get a draw, and that is just what their intentions were that night. They packed midfield and played with Jamie Hoyland as a sweeper with one man up front. Their tactics were to frustrate us, but it didn't work and Keano saw to that. He seemed to have half of Ireland over to see his home début and scored twice in 3–0 win.

Roy picked up a booking when Tom Cowan conned the ref. into thinking he had been fouled, and there were also yellow cards for five Sheffield players, but it was not a rough-house.

The first goal came after 17 minutes when Ryan back-headed the ball into Roy's path, and he got a second just before half-time ramming in a low shot, after Sparky took control with that broad chest of his and rolled a perfect pass.

There were plenty of smiles in the dressing-room at half time and we felt that we had the game in the bag. I played until the 70th minute when Brian McClair took over. We got our third thanks to the speed of Giggsy when he set off on a great run and did everything right. He beat the Sheffield defence and pulled the cross over for Mark Hughes to force it home.

Two games played, both won and two clean sheets. Not a bad start.

What a contrast to the previous year when after two games we were bottom of the table with five goals against and just one to our credit and without a single point. If we could win the championship after that start, what could we do this time?

We had ambitions to succeed in another area too, and realized that the better we could do in the early stages of the season the more it would help us later. We wanted to get beyond the knock-out stage of the European Champions' Cup, knowing only too well that if we did it could take its toll. We would be faced with a packed fixture list but we were prepared for it.

Tiredness, injuries, possible suspensions and whatever else the season might throw up could hit our chances – so a good start was essential. The bigger the lead, the more we could cushion ourselves if or when form slipped, or if there was a fixture pile-up.

A lot has been said about the size of the Premiership and steps are being taken to reduce the number of teams, but the sooner we get down to 18 the better. Having to play 42 League matches, plus domestic cup games and then perhaps another 10 European games, is too much. It is ridiculous to be expected to compete on equal terms with foreign sides who have played far fewer games – and the sooner the authorities do something about it the better.

The boss made it clear that he wanted to protect me as much as possible from the demands of a long season. He thought three games in seven days was too much. If they were I didn't notice. With two already under my belt I was ready for anything, but those results could have helped a little!

Before a ball was kicked the bookies had made us favourites to win the championship again. After two wins the odds were coming down, although none of us had put any money on ourselves. That is one thing we would never do.

Most of the lads like a flutter and many of us do the fixed odds pools during the week, but it is a dressing-room rule, probably founded on superstition, that we never bet on Manchester United.

We talked about the threat of the opposition and who our main challengers might be, but by the time the second Saturday of the season came along you could hardly say that a clear picture was emerging. Each club had played two games. We had won both our fixtures and four other sides also had 100 per cent records – Liverpool, Everton, Coventry and Ipswich.

As for Arsenal, Blackburn and Villa – all three of them dropped points in the first week. Norwich pulled off a surprise by beating Blackburn 3–2 at Ewood Park three days after we won at Carrow Road, Arsenal came back from that upset by Coventry to beat Spurs 1–0; then Villa drew at Hillsborough after their opening home win.

Some of the lads fancied Liverpool and Leeds as main contenders, but nobody mentioned Ipswich who were up with the front-runners in that early sprint away from the starting line.

So came our second home game and my third start. I would have been choked if I had been left out because it was Newcastle – the club I supported when I was a boy – who came to Old Trafford for our first Saturday fixture of the season.

We drew – and the boss was a far from happy man when he came into the dressing-room afterwards. He had a real go. He said we had defended terribly and that we had let our standards slip.

'The only exceptions are Incey and Robbo,' he said. 'They are the only two who have come out with any credit today.'

The dressing-room was fairly quiet for a few minutes but I was satisfied that at least I had shown I could play three games in seven days. This time I had been left on for the whole 90 minutes, with Brian McClair replacing Andrei 20 minutes from time and Lee Sharpe taking over from Paul Parker just before the end.

Don't get me wrong, the gaffer didn't storm into us, throwing tea-cups around the dressing-room. Those days are long gone. He has calmed down a lot since he first came to the club. The lads know him and how to approach him and he knows all his players.

I can understand why he used to fly off the handle. He is a perfectionist and it was a way of getting rid of his frustration when things did not go according to plan. He is fully aware of every player's capabilities and only criticizes when he feels that the standard is dropping, but he generally does it in a fair way. As long as a player gives him the kind of performance he expects, there is no reason to demonstrate the Ferguson temper.

Newcastle took full marks from me as far as their approach to the game was concerned, but I suppose it was nothing more than we should have expected from a side managed by Kevin Keegan. I played with Kevin at England level and we have kept in touch over the years, and I know what he is trying to achieve at Newcastle. He has done a fantastic job so far and everyone on Tyneside is pleased with the way he has pulled them out of the Second Division to build a side capable of challenging the best.

I have seen it happen in football before and it is strange how success can snowball. Leeds did it when they were promoted and carried on winning in the then First Division. When I spoke to the Newcastle lads after the game I realized that they also expected to do well, but deep down I thought they still had a bit of a way to go.

They played some nice bright football and tried to make a game of it. Norwich and Sheffield United had decided that the best way to play us was to defend, Newcastle's policy was the opposite. They passed the ball about, and even though we went ahead when Giggsy scored just before half-time, they kept on playing and were rewarded with an equalizer.

It was a bit of a jolt for us. Normally if we go one up at home it is the key to more goals but not this time. They played to Kevin's plan and who else but Andy Cole popped up to score.

I cannot believe why Andy has been criticized by some of our so-called experts. They say that he is not an all-round player but who can deny his goal-scoring ability? I cannot pay him a bigger compliment than to say that his style of play reminds me of Gary Lineker. He is a lethal finisher who plays on defenders' shoulders. He is always trying to catch them on the turn as he runs in behind and that is just what he did to Steve Bruce.

Newcastle broke down the left wing and slipped the ball through. Cole ran around behind Steve and chipped big Peter Schmeichel to score the first goal we had given away in 250 minutes of football. It was the mark of a great finisher.

Of the three teams we had faced, Newcastle looked by far the best although that draw at Old Trafford had given them their first point. I know Norwich had pushed us during 1992–93 but they seemed to have little new to offer. Chris Sutton was emerging as a quality player but would they keep him at Carrow Road?

Sheffield United looked as though they would have a battle to stay up even so early in the season, and while I have a soft spot for Newcastle I honestly did not think at that stage that they were going to be any sort of a threat. I felt that Kevin still had work to do especially in strengthening his defence.

But it was our defenders who were the target of criticism after that home draw.

With three games played and seven points in the bag we came to our second major test of the season. It was Aston Villa's turn to try and stop us improving on our already reasonable start.

That was a game I would dearly have loved to play in and face the challenge of my old boss Ron Atkinson. I have plenty of friends at Villa Park, including my former team-mate Paul McGrath. On top of that I have always enjoyed playing against Villa because they were one of our local rivals during my days at West Brom.

But no, a certain referee's report saw to it that I missed the next two games through suspension. That pre-season sending off in Johannesburg meant I spent the evening working for Sky TV rather than being out there on the field. My only consolation was that it was a brilliant game to watch.

Four matches into the season and our second time on live television. We were certainly being put under the microscope although at that stage it was our skills which were being highlighted. As the months went by we found ourselves subjected to a trial by TV, but I will come to that later.

It was a big disappointment not being involved, but as so often happens in football, one player's misfortune leads to another's good luck. My suspension meant Lee Sharpe could get back into the side after being on the bench for the first three games.

He had a blinder, no doubt inspired by the fact that he was playing against the club he supported when he was a kid, and he seemed determined to show the boss that he wanted to stay in the starting line-up. He scored both our goals either side of an equalizer from Dalian Atkinson in a game full of flowing movement and skill.

I was obviously delighted that we came out winners and that we had picked up three more points, but there was more to it than that. Both our goals were stunning, the whole country had seen them and those bookmakers' odds dropped a bit more. We were at the top of the table playing superb football and as I sat there in the television studio I wondered if I would ever get my place back!

If you are in a side that is playing well and you get on the scoresheet it makes it very difficult for the manager to drop you. If you are sitting on the sidelines watching other people doing the business then you know that you have a fight on your hands to get back into the team.

We had regarded Villa as the first real test. I mean no disrespect to Norwich but it was Big Ron's boys who had given us the hardest fight on the way to the title, and to beat them the way we did was totally satisfying.

Sharpey's performance guaranteed his place for the trip to Southampton as I served out the other half of my South African sentence, and Eric Cantona was back too.

Back? He was brilliant. Some of our critics say that we rely too much on Eric. We have proved them wrong time and again and no more so than in those opening four games when he was missing.

It is not a total reliance on one man. We are not that kind of a team. But I have to admit that when Eric is present and playing at the top of his game he makes the whole unit blend. At The Dell he created two goals and scored the other with a superb chip that must have had Matt Le Tissier drooling.

A one-man team? Surely one of our strengths in recent years is that we have been anything but. We have different 'star men' every week and this was clearly illustrated in those opening games.

At Norwich Mark Hughes was magnificent, against Sheffield United it was Roy Keane, then at Villa Park Lee Sharpe put in a tremendous performance. Six days later the spotlight had swung in Eric's direction.

That is the secret of our success. We play as a team but we also have some superb soloists to call upon when circumstances demand it.

We had already been tested by one of the previous season's promotion sides and were due to face a second as I made my come-back from the two-match ban. West Ham had helped to spoil our push for the title in 1992 when, just a few days after they had been relegated, they pulled off a surprise by beating us 1-0.

This time at Old Trafford they had little to offer. It never looked as if they would score and we finished up with a comfortable 3-0 win. I managed to get on for the last 20 minutes because Andrei Kanchelskis had to come off. He picked up a slight strain but it was no surprise. He had given Julian Dicks such a run-around he was probably exhausted, and I am sure the Hammers' full back, who later joined Liverpool, was glad to see the back of him.

The boss was happy because we had given a good solid performance, and Lee Sharpe found himself wearing the mantle of leading scorer after getting his fourth goal in three games. Nobody had mentioned him when we were talking about who might top the chart!

Six games played, five wins and one draw. The newspapers were full of talk about us retaining the title. We said nothing.

I know I have made it clear that trying to hold on to the Premiership trophy was our aim but the players kept their thoughts to themselves. There is no surer way of guaranteeing that you will fall flat on your face when you go out onto an ice-rink than to tell everyone what a wonderful skater you are!

Talking about what we might do is not our style although sometimes when you pick up your newspaper you could be forgiven for thinking that we had been shooting our mouths off. Nobody at Old Trafford had made any claims about what we hoped to win, and to the best of my knowledge during my time at the club nobody ever did.

But when you see headlines like, 'Catch us if you can!' it must give people the impression that it is the players or the manager who are making that claim – until you read the story. Then you discover some sportswriter is probably asking 'Just who is going to stop Manchester United?'

The answer to that came at Stamford Bridge when Chelsea beat us 1–0. It was our first defeat of the season but I can assure you it was one which hurt.

I am not going to make any excuses but the game came at the end of a week when virtually all our players had been on international duty and we paid a price for our success. We looked a bit jaded and I felt that we never reached 100 per cent. It was no surprise after the demands made during the week and the travelling involved. Tiredness crept in and some of the lads could only manage what I would call a 95 per cent performance, good enough to beat some sides but not Chelsea that afternoon.

We also played without Mark Hughes. Our European campaign was due to begin four days later and the boss decided to field the side he would play in Hungary when we faced Kispest Honved in Budapest. During our UEFA Cup-tie against Torpedo Moscow the previous season Sparky had been sent off following two bookable offences, and because of this had to serve a one-match ban.

It saved the gaffer a headache because he would have had to leave out one of his regular starters for a major game because of what we all feel is a crazy rule. English clubs are heavily handicapped by UEFA's 'foreigner' restriction, which limits the number of non-English players a team can field.

Non-English means just that. Welsh, Scottish, and Irish players are bracketed with anyone from as far away as Australia or Afghanistan. With a Danish goalkeeper, a Ukrainian right-winger and a French striker we perhaps suffer more than most.

The daft thing is that Sparky, who was born about 40 miles from Manchester, and Ryan Giggs, who has spent more or less the whole of his life in Salford five minutes from Old Trafford, are both hit by the ruling. They are classed not as foreigners but as 'assimilated' players, which is simply another way of saying that they are placed under some sort of restriction.

The rule would be understandable if it applied simply to those players who did not have a British passport but there are political implications behind it. Many see it as an attempt to pressurize this country into forming a British team to represent us at international level rather than having the four-nations set-up.

I cannot see that ever happening because the four governing Football Associations of England, Scotland, Wales and Northern Ireland would strongly oppose any kind of amalgamation. However, I am sure that if a British team ever did represent us in competitions such as the World Cup we could come up with quite a line-up. Then they would probably want to change the rule back again!

Sparky stood down for the game at Stamford Bridge and we played with Roy Keane wide on the right in place of Andrei Kanchelskis.

Play? For the first quarter of an hour we were hardly in the game. Then luck went Chelsea's way.

Eric Cantona picked up the ball from a clearance and saw that their goalkeeper, Dmitri Kharine, was stranded. For a moment it was France versus Russia and it looked as though Monsieur Cantona was a sure winner. He chipped Kharine even though he was just inside the Chelsea half and I thought he had scored a wonder goal.

But the ball took a mighty bounce, hit the crossbar and rebounded into the 'keeper's hands as he chased back towards his line! I cannot remember seeing anything like that before and it summed up our luck that afternoon.

In fairness to Chelsea they had made most of the running in those opening stages, and from Kharine's clearance kick they got their reward. The ball went through to Steve Clarke who hit a low shot which Peter Schmeichel could only palm away. Gavin Peacock was following up and got in first. It is not very often that those big Danish hands let the ball slip, but this time it rebounded into Peacock's path and we conceded our fourth goal of the season.

In the second half we fought hard and I thought that we did enough to get a point. But we went down 1–0 for our first league defeat since Oldham had beaten us at Boundary Park by an identical scoreline just before we started our run-in to the championship six months earlier.

Our record of sixteen Premiership games without losing was ended. It was hardly the best way to prepare for a major European game. There was nothing we could do about it though, and two days later we boarded the flight for Budapest.

To say that we enjoyed the trip to Hungary would be a bit of an exaggeration. I know modern-day footballers should be quite used to jumping on a plane and nipping off here, there and everywhere but there are some of the lads who hate it.

We quite often fly to league games at places like Norwich or Southampton, and while this can save hours against travelling by coach it does have its disadvantages. Eric Cantona, Ryan Giggs, Paul Ince and Gary Pallister are all terrified. They absolutely hate it and I think that if the boss gave them a choice they would rather walk!

For domestic fixtures there is an option, but not for international and European fixtures. I am certain that the nervous tension used up during a flight drains the lads so the manager has to do his best to counteract this. He organizes our European trips so that we are there for as long as possible before the game but gets us home as quickly as possible afterwards. That might mean flying out on a Monday for a Wednesday match and returning in the early hours of the Thursday morning, but it can be worth it.

The fear of flying is something the lads have had to overcome but the rest of us know that they go through hell every time we step on board an aircraft. On the flight to Hungary they were not alone.

We were on a smaller plane than the type the club normally charters for European trips, and because of this were unable to fly above the level of turbulence. We were thrown around a lot and our stomachs were churning by the time we touched down. Even the most experienced travellers felt a bit queezie and there were some green-tinted faces, especially amongst the Press corps – although that could have been down to the in-flight drinks!

For us Hungary was familiar territory. We had been there several times during my days at the club and when the draw for the first round was announced wondered if our luck was in. In 1990 our first-round tie in the Cup-Winners' Cup was against the Hungarian side Pecsi Munkas and we went on to lift the trophy. Could the same happen again?

Budapest is a beautiful city and we stayed in a first-class hotel. The weather was kind and it gave us a chance to relax and do some sight-seeing which put us in a great frame of mind for the game. Eric, Paul, Ryan and Gary got their feet back on the ground, so they were settled and everything was ready.

There had been some speculation that the game might be switched to the Nep Stadium, Hungary's equivalent of Wembley, because the local media had given the tie such a big build-up. But the evening before, when we went for our training session we found it was being played in Honved's own stadium which is much smaller and a bit basic in facilities.

We were hundreds of miles from home in an East European country and as we ran out for training what greeted us?

'Champions! Champions!' Our supporters had got there before us. They are an incredible bunch and will turn up in their hundreds even to watch us prepare for a game. Many of them spend every penny they have to get to faraway places and the players truly appreciate the effort they put in.

As for Honved, our younger players learned about the leading role the club has played in football history. It was their players who formed the backbone to the famous Hungarian side which helped to transform the game in the 1950s. The Magnificent Magyars came to Wembley to beat England 6–3 in 1953, and a year later beat us again 7–1 in a World Cup qualifying game in Budapest.

I'm glad I wasn't around at that time! Can you imagine the headlines if that sort of thing happened today?

The great Ferenc Puskas was part of that side and he was there to welcome us when we got to Budapest. There is a strong link between the Hungarian star and United because after the 1956 uprising in his country Puskas went to Spain and joined Real Madrid, who became one of our biggest rivals in the days when the famous Busby Babes had striven for success in the European Cup.

The Hungarians love their football and on the evening of the game we faced a partisan crowd as we took United's first step in the Champions Cup for a quarter of a century. It was at that moment that it came home to many of us how immense a task it was and how important a competition this was.

'Champions! Champions!' Every club has qualified by winning its national championship and every supporter has the right to chant that war cry. The entrants represent the top sides from virtually every European nation. We knew what we had gone through to take the title and we were up against players who had done the same. This would be no easy passage.

The gaffer's team selection had to take into account the UEFA restrictions, so Big Peter was in goal, using up one of our foreign places, and the others were taken by Eric and Roy Keane. We were allowed two assimilated players, so Denis Irwin and Ryan were able to play, but there was no room for Andrei Kanchelskis or Brian McClair.

An assimilated player is one who has played all his professional football in the country of the club he represents. Denis was born in the Irish Republic but joined Leeds when he was a youngster and went through the ranks before moving to Oldham, then eventually to Old Trafford. He has played all his football in England, and the same applies to Ryan who has been with United since his school days.

I was one of the English contingent along with Paul Parker, Steve Bruce, Gary Pallister, Lee Sharpe and Paul Ince and on the bench were Micky Phelan, Dion Dublin, Les Sealey, Lee Martin and young Nicky Butt – all Englishmen.

We got off to the perfect start when Roy Keane scored after 8 minutes after a good run from Giggsy. The Hungarians hit back and equalized just before half-time through Josef Szabados, and I think the home side were willing to settle for the scores being level at the break.

Not us. Two minutes after the Honved equalizer Roy got his second and within a minute Eric made it 3–1. What a perfect way to end your first 45 minutes in the European Cup.

When we got into the dressing-room at half-time the boss was delighted. His instructions for the second half were to keep it simple, stick to our shape and make sure that we gave nothing away at the back.

We did what he said . . . for 20 minutes! Then came a daft goal.

Istvan Stefanov chipped big Peter from the edge of the box. We were 3–2 up yet we found ourselves hanging on.

In the end we won, and knew that those three away goals would put us in a strong position for the second leg.

That was a fortnight off and before it we had two home games in the Premiership and a tricky Coca-Cola Cup tie.

The television cameras were on us again as we beat Arsenal at Old Trafford. I was out of the side and saw Eric score a superb goal with a tremendous shot.

Paul Ince had been obstructed during a run at goal and the referee gave us an indirect free kick a few yards outside the box. Arsenal formed their wall, Incey touched the ball to Eric and he bent it beautifully beyond the reach of Dave Seaman. That meant three more valuable points.

	P	W	D	L	F	A	PTS
Manchester United	8	6	1	1	15	4	19
Arsenal	8	5	1	2	11	6	16
Aston Villa	8	4	3	1	11	6	15
Everton	8	5	0	3	10	6	15

So the team I regarded as our biggest threat was in second place and one of the other favourites lay third. Blackburn were eighth, Leeds ninth and Liverpool tenth but it was early days.

The line-up against Arsenal was more or less back to what it had been before the Chelsea upset. Mark Hughes led the attack for all but the last minute. Then he came off and Brian McClair took over with Andrei Kanchelskis watching a little disappointedly from the bench. Andrei is an international and was not too happy about being left out of the side. I could sympathize with him, nobody wants to spend match days watching others playing, and he made it clear that he wanted to be out there too.

He got his chance three days later when we went to Stoke for the Coca-Cola game and showed the kind of form which would make a tremendous impact on our season. The side we fielded at the Victoria Ground caused an uproar even though I am certain that Alex was dead right doing what he did.

It is impossible to pick and choose which competitions you want to win. You know that you have to try your best in all of them. However, the manager felt that at this stage of this particular competition, against opposition from a lower league, he could use his squad to its full extent.

We lined up: Schmeichel, Martin, Irwin, Phelan, Pallister, Ferguson, Robson, Kanchelskis, McClair, Hughes, and Dublin. No Paul Parker, no Eric Cantona, no Paul Ince, no Ryan Giggs and no Roy Keane.

The Stoke supporters made their feelings known. Before the game there were protests, with 23,000 fans yelling their anger when the names were read out. Some of them saw it as a rip-off because they had paid to see the missing stars. Others said it was an insult to their side.

What a load of rubbish. The manager was not taking a gamble, he was simply using some players who were not regular starters in the first leg of a cup tie. If the issue was being decided over one game he might have viewed things differently. There were few protests from the Stoke fans when we lost 2–1!

Look at the facts. We were trying to make a challenge on several fronts and everyone at the club knew that if we were successful we would have to play around 70 games. Nobody can do that with fourteen or fifteen players. Alex's policy was to rest key members of the squad whenever possible and make sure they were ready for vital games.

We would have liked to have held Stoke to a draw rather than end the game a goal down, but it was not to be thanks to the striking skills of Mark Stein. He scored two beauties and his performance probably did a lot to influence Chelsea's million-pound move for him a short time later.

The papers had a bit of a go at us the next day, but the boss stood firm and he proved he was right as the season went on and the demands grew. Lou Macari, who was manager of Stoke at the time, was totally on Alex's side. In fact he said he hoped we would field our youth team in the second leg!

Lou was only joking – he knows the youth side would have stretched anybody! And while I am on the subject of joking I have got to mention what happened after that game.

I suppose I should have been ready for it having played alongside the 'wee man' when he was at Old Trafford, but as I got dressed after my shower I pulled on one of my socks, and pulled, and pulled. It went over my foot and kept going up to my knee. Gary Pallister had the same problem.

Louie had struck. He had cut the toes out while we were on the field! It is one of his favourite tricks but it was nowhere near as bad as the time a team of English football writers had played a friendly against some Italian journalists at The Cliff.

It was during Ron Atkinson's reign when we were due to face Juventus in a European game the next day. Louie sabotaged all their socks and they found the snipped-off toes at the bottom of the teapot *after* they had their post-match drink. Some of them even commented that it was the best cup of tea they had ever tasted!

During the Stoke game Andrei performed well, earning his place in the team for the start of the Premiership clash with Swindon. The Wiltshire side had got off to a terrible start. It was the season's ninth league game but by the time they came to Old Trafford we had a 16 point lead over them and they were still looking for their first win.

Andrei was out to show that he deserved a regular place and brought the crowd to its feet in the 4th minute when he scored a super goal. He picked up the ball somewhere around the half-way line and ran at goal with his amazing speed before slipping it under the 'keeper.

I missed the 4–2 win, but I think Andrei made his point. Even so the boss left him out of second leg of the European game as Honved came to Old Trafford, but it was simply because of the 'foreigner' rule as we reverted to formation number three! It seemed that we now had three first teams – one for the Premiership, another for the Coca-Cola Cup and the third for Europe.

There was a slight change. Mark Hughes was back after his ban, so Roy Keane stepped down.

We had the one-goal cushion from the first leg and, coupled to the three away goals, were favourites to go through. Nevertheless the boss demanded tightness in defence.

I don't think he expected the defenders to contribute to the goals as well but that is what happened. Steve Bruce scored two beauties, both headers which brought back memories of the previous season when he struck twice against Sheffield Wednesday. We gave away a late goal but by that time the tie was beyond Honved's reach and we found ourselves bang on course as far as our pre-season priorities were concerned.

Three days later the fans were gathering at The Cliff as they waited for news of the second-round draw. There were plenty of glamour names involved: AC Milan, Barcelona, Feyenoord, and Monaco who had replaced the disgraced French champions Marseille who were banned because of a bribes scandal.

And who did we get? Porto? Steaua Bucharest? Werder Bremen?

No. Galatasaray, champions of Turkey.

On paper it looked like a tie we should win but we all knew that football is never as simple as that. I seemed to be the only one who knew anything about them because I had played against Galatasaray about thirteen years earlier during my time at West Brom. I knew they would have changed a bit since those days, when we won 2–0 in Istanbul and 3–0 at The Hawthorns, but I could give the lads some idea of what to expect.

There has been a marked improvement in Turkish football over the years, especially since my early days at international level when England would overrun them. Victories of 8–0 and 5–0 were commonplace. Then it became harder and the scorelines reduced until the last time we played against them at Wembley and we only managed a 1–0 victory.

The introduction of German coaching and a growing interest in the game in Turkey had brought about the changes, and we knew that Galatasaray might not be the walkover many of the back-page experts were predicting.

CHAPTER THREE
Turkish Despair – 'Derby' Delight

I THINK IT IS FAIR TO SAY THAT THE MAJORITY OF OUR supporters expected us to have a reasonably easy passage against Galatasaray. Most people felt we should be capable of moving through to the lucrative league section of the Champions' Cup – where groups of four clubs play one another on a home and away basis.

In the dressing-room we were more cautious, knowing that football at this level cannot be easy, but at the same time we realized that we could have been facing tougher opponents.

Leeds had fallen at this stage of the competition the previous season, when they were knocked out by Glasgow Rangers, but surely the Turks would not pose that kind of threat for us? Little did we suspect the traumas that would accompany the second-round tie.

Before facing Galatasaray we had three domestic fixtures and I found myself involved in two of them.

I missed the first. The 3–2 win against Sheffield Wednesday at Hillsborough when the fans saw a five-goal second-half as once again we took maximum points from my old mate Trevor Francis. Clashes between our two clubs have provided some superb games in recent seasons, none more spectacular than the thriller at Old Trafford during our 1993 championship run-in when we came back from one down to win in time-added thanks to two Steve Bruce headers.

The Hillsborough game was the first since that vitally important afternoon and after a goal-less first half we found ourselves trailing again. Chris Bart-Williams scored when Wednesday caught us unawares with a quickly taken free kick.

The shock was just what we needed and it brought the best out of our attack. In the next 20 minutes we took a grip of the game and I knew that we would not let go. Mark Hughes scored twice and Ryan Giggs added a third. Eric Cantona had a hand in both the second and third goals and once again must have made Wednesday rue the day when they let him slip through their fingers. Mark Bright popped one in two minutes from time to give the home fans some hope, but we cruised in to retain our lead at the top.

Then came the second leg of our League Cup tie against Stoke and we were determined that it was going to be a different story this time. The boss changed our line-up slightly but this time without any complaints from the Stoke fans. They fancied their side's chances of getting through and were not too bothered that some of the big names were missing.

I think the moans at the Victoria ground came because a lot of people who do not normally go to games had bought tickets to see Eric Cantona and Ryan Giggs in action. These were the players who were regularly stealing the headlines and I suppose for them to be left out must have been a disappointment. But I agreed totally with the boss's thinking. He knew where his priorities lay and with a squad the size of ours he was determined to give every player a chance and use it to its fullest extent.

He had made it clear to us that the 'Coca-Cola' was the least important of the four competitions we were involved in although he also emphasized the importance of winning. There was no way he wanted us to go out at such an early stage.

The Stoke fans got one of their wishes as Ryan was in the squad and Steve Bruce and Lee Sharpe who had been on the bench for the first game were also starters. Roy Keane had also missed out at the Victoria Ground but at Old Trafford he played the whole 90 minutes, and I lined up alongside him because Paul Ince was injured.

We were ready to show that the first-leg result was a one-off but the opening 45 minutes failed to produce a goal.

'Keep it going and the goals will come', was the boss's message at the break, and he was right. A minute into the second half and Andrei Kanchelskis went on one of his powerful sprints down the right wing. He pulled over a cross and Lee Sharpe hit in a terrific volley to put us in front.

It was 2–2 on aggregate and even though we felt comfortable we did not get the winner until extra time was just two minutes away. Mark Hughes picked up a loose ball which bounced off Toddy Orlygsson, the former Nottingham Forest player, and hit a pass for Brian McClair who struck a firm left-foot shot to take us through to round three.

Then came a ten-day gap between fixtures because of World Cup qualifying games, and the players who went off on international duty left us with a diminished pool as we carried on with our daily training routine at The Cliff.

It felt strange for me. After all those years of being a regular member of the England team it was still difficult to adjust to not being part of the set-up. I have to admit that I felt a few pangs of regret whenever the squad was announced, not because I was no longer involved, but for the simple reason that I felt I still had something to offer at international level.

I knew that I was good enough to do a job for England but Graham Taylor had made it clear that I was no longer a part of his plans. That made me all the more determined to perform well at club level.

It was after we had finished one of our morning sessions when the news reached us that Jim Holton had died. Big Jim was United's centre-half during the early seventies when Tommy Docherty was manager so there were plenty of people at the club who knew him well. He was much more than that to me. He was a close friend I had known for more than twenty years.

Jim was a huge, warm, friendly bloke whom I first met when I was a young lad starting my career with West Brom. He was the first-team centre-half and he and his wife Jan virtually adopted me. They would to take me for days out, visits to the zoo or the cinema and would invite me to their home for meals. Jim treated me like a younger brother.

He was a great favourite with the Old Trafford fans and he and Jan were very popular in Coventry where they had success in the pub trade after Jim ended his playing days. He had died from a heart attack after going on a training run. I was stunned.

Two days before our next game the squad was back to full strength as the players who had been on international duty returned from their various trips. Andrei and Peter were due back 24 hours later but the boss had already included them in his plans for the Saturday home clash with Tottenham. I was playing too because Incey was still injured.

It was one of those games I felt we would win comfortably because we seemed to be in control from the start. We took the lead through Roy Keane who scored his fifth of the season with a low, powerful shot from just around the edge of the penalty area. The goal came after Lee Sharpe created the chance with a good cross from the left wing.

That is one of the strong points of Lee's game. He rarely wastes a cross and I reckon that even though injury robbed him of a regular place in the England side, and he found himself being played out of position by Graham Taylor, we have yet to see the best of him.

He has been at Old Trafford since the well-catalogued time when the boss and Archie Knox did a bit of moonlighting in Torquay. They apparently signed Lee in the early hours of the morning. He was just a kid who had played a handful of games for the seaside club, yet they were determined to get their 'man' and stuck to the task after receiving some glowing reports about him.

At the time the gaffer said he was taking a gamble but it was one which has paid off. Lee has reached the top the hard way though. He has been forced to overcome some major upsets which might have proved too much for anyone with less determination.

Each time the ladder has been pulled away from under him, he has got back on it and progressed to a higher rung than where he left off. I am certain that in the next two or three years we will see him become an outstanding player and hopefully there will be no more setbacks.

Twice he has had hernia operations but the biggest blow was when he went down with viral meningitis. He was ill for the whole of one summer and it kept him out of action for a good three months of the 1992–93 season. He gets full marks for the way he has battled back.

He did what many top players have had to do when they find themselves out of the game through injury or illness. He showed a determination to get himself fit again. Training alone, especially in a gymnasium with nothing for company but the radio, can be make or break time for a player. If he gives in and lounges around, perhaps doing only part of the fitness programme which has been worked out for him by the physio, he will start on the downward spiral which leads nowhere.

I can speak from experience when I say that it takes a lot of concentration and effort. During my career I have had some long lonely hours running around the perimeter of the training pitch or pumping away on the gymnasium apparatus, but it is all worthwhile in the end. This is a part of football people outside the game know little about and it is far removed from all the glamour of running out at Wembley in front of a full house.

There is not one top player who has not had to go through the frustration of the solo training session, and I have seen what happens to those who refuse to knuckle down and accept the hard work. It would be unfair to name names but I have seen many promising lads who could be playing at the top today if only they had been able to discipline themselves into working hard like the rest of us.

It may sound corny but there is no easy way to the top. Lee has discovered that early in his career and I am confident he will reap the rewards. Certainly during our push to retain the title Sharpey played a vital part, never more so than during that Tottenham game when three minutes after making one goal he scored the second. It came from a mistake by David Howells in the Spurs midfield. The ball went spinning off him and into Lee's path. He hit it home and we looked comfortable with a 2–0 lead.

The boss decided to give Brian McClair part of a game and took me off. No sooner had he done this than Darren Caskey pulled a goal back for Tottenham after a bit of confusion in our defence. Surely we would not let things slip at this stage?

No, we still had control despite the upset. Nicky Butt replaced Ryan Giggs with eleven minutes to go and that added a bit of youthful enthusiasm to our midfield. Nicky is a player who will not hold back from a challenge and there are many aspects of his game which remind me of someone I know well. Me!

It was another of our midfielders who took the spotlight that day. I thought it was Roy Keane's best showing since his arrival from Forest. He was outstanding and did enough to convince the gaffer that he should be in the line-up for the Galatasaray game which came along four days later.

Because of this one of our 'foreigner' places was taken, big Peter used up another and Eric the third.

We had problems. Paul Parker went down with flu, and that was no help to the manager's planning because Parks was one of our English contingent. He knew we could use two assimilated players in addition to the three foreigners so the boss opted for the Welshmen Mark Hughes and Ryan Giggs, which meant there was no room for Denis Irwin. Lee Sharpe dropped back to cover the left full-back position and Lee Martin was drafted into the back four.

The manager had been on a spying mission to Turkey. He had also studied videos and read through the reports from other members of the backroom staff who had flown out to see Galatasaray in action. In his team talk he told us that they had some useful players, but we still felt confident that we would be able to beat them.

There was one surprise for us before the game had even started. I thought we would have a full house for that first leg and we were a bit disappointed with the Old Trafford crowd which was just under 40,000. I suppose there were several reasons for this.

Firstly, the tie was being shown 'live' on ITV, which meant there would be more viewers than for a regular satellite screening. Then we had to consider the attraction of the opposition:

The summer of '93 and sunshine in Soweto as a future member of the England coaching staff gets in some practice. *Empics/Phil O'Brien*

A big-two summit. Nelson Mandela, later to be elected President of South Africa, meets Ryan Giggs during the pre-season tour. *Empics/Phil O'Brien*

I was not too happy to be sent off during the friendly against Arsenal in South Africa. The red card led to a two-match ban back in England once the season started. *Empics/Phil O'Brien*

The pre-season friendly against Celtic, and Paul McStay prepares to hand over the traditional pennant watched by referee Roger Milford. Note the officials' strip. Because we wore our new black-and-gold away gear, the referee and linesmen were in red and white. *Empics/Neal Simpson*

The Charity Shield at Wembley and a tussle for the ball with Arsenal's Paul Merson. *Action Images*

Andrei Kanchelskis leads the lap of honour after the Charity Shield victory over Arsenal. The game ended 1-1 after 90 minutes with United winning the penalty shoot-out 5-4. *Action Images*

Goal number 97. Our second of the season in the opening game against Norwich at Carrow Road, and one which gave me a great deal of pleasure. It kept me level with Giggsy in the goals chart for six whole days! *Action Images*

Newcastle's goal-scoring enigma Andy Cole, in action against us at Old Trafford. Kevin Keegan's side managed a 1-1 draw in both encounters, with Handy Andy scoring each time. *Empics/Graham Chadwick*

Chelsea were the only side with a 100 per cent record against us in the League during the 1993-94 season, winning 1-0 at Stamford Bridge and Old Trafford. Here I get a header in despite the efforts of Frank Sinclair as our first defeat looms. *Action Images*

Steve Bruce in his Geronimo outfit in discussion with Peter Schmeichel: 'We had Chinese last week, what about a pizza tonight?' Bruised and battered, Brucie managed to stay the course for our 1-0 win over Arsenal at Old Trafford. *Empics/Ross Kinnaird*

The perfect start to our European Champions' Cup game against Galatasaray as, with just three minutes gone, I managed to score. What a pity the second-round tie went downhill from then on. *Empics/Rui Vieira*

The inhabitants of 'The Hell'. Life can be fun in the Alisamiyen Stadium in Istanbul, but not for the visitors. This was the scene before our second-leg clash with Galatasaray in the Champions' Cup as the Turks prepared to welcome us. *Action Images*

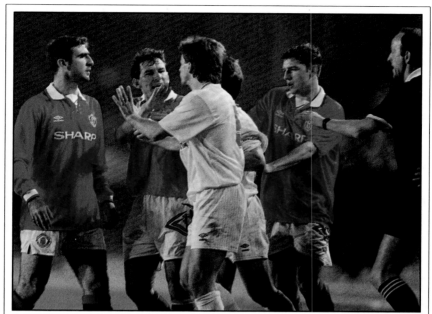

The trouble starts. Eric Cantona is surrounded by Galatasaray players after accusing them of time-wasting tactics. The second-leg ended 0-0 and we were out of Europe thanks to the 'away goals' rule. *Empics/Ross Kinnaird*

All hell lets loose in 'The Hell'. Eric Cantona protests after being struck by a policeman, Paul Parker is pushed down the steps that lead to the dressing rooms and I find myself in the thick of things. I still wonder what would have happened if our police had attacked the Turkish players in this way. *Empics/Ross Kinnaird*

Steve Hodge slides in during the goalless draw against Leeds on New Year's Day 1994.
Action Images

Old Trafford in total silence. United and Everton players and officials stand in line after being led on to the field by a lone piper. This was the poignant scene shortly before kick-off, two days after the death of club president, Sir Matt Busby. *Empics/Phil O'Brien*

Galatasaray were not exactly an AC Milan or a Barcelona who could field sides full of big-name stars. The Turks were an unknown quantity as far as our supporters were concerned, and when you add to all this the cost of watching modern-day football, perhaps 39,346 was a reasonable turn out.

Whatever the attendance there was no way we could have asked for a better start. The game was only three minutes old when Roy Keane and Eric Cantona were involved in a combination of passes down our left flank. The ball was played into the box and I saw the opening, ran onto it and we were one up!

Old Trafford exploded. Although I didn't know it at the time, that was to be my last European goal for Manchester United. I only wish that it could have taken us beyond the second round.

Things got better before they got worse! Ten minutes later we won a corner and as Ryan Giggs floated the ball in, Gary Pallister pressurized their big centre-forward Sukur Hakan who was helping out in defence. The Turk tried to head the ball out to safety but all he did was put it beyond the reach of his goalkeeper. It was a great goal . . . but not quite what he intended.

Thirteen minutes gone and we were 2–0 ahead. We were on cloud nine, the crowd wanted more goals and I can imagine how the Turks felt.

There they were, hundreds of miles from home in front of a crowd that was really getting behind the home side, and with over an hour still to play they were trailing. Not only that, they had scored one of those goals themselves. Psychologically we had the game won; it would have been the end for many teams. Not Galatasaray.

The last thing we needed was for them to get any kind of break which would boost their sagging morale, but it came. They moved forward in the 16th minute and as I went into a challenge the ball broke loose. I thought we might get to it first but Arif Erdem ran through and hit one of those shots footballers dream about. He was 25 yards out but the ball flew into the top corner beyond Peter Schmeichel. Galatasaray were back in the game and that turned out to be the turning-point of the tie.

If we could have kept the score at 2–0 for another quarter of an hour or so, I am sure the Turks would have collapsed and we would have chalked up a big win. The goal gave them confidence and they came at us again and again and in the 32nd minute scored an equalizer.

Lee Martin turned to hit a back pass towards goal but he miskicked and the ball went away from Peter Schmeichel, who had come to the edge of his area to play it away. It would have rolled into our net even if Kubilay had not latched onto it.

Poor Lee was devastated. I felt sorry for the lad because it seemed that luck was stacked against him. He had been a regular in the side in the 1989–90 season and it was his goal in the FA Cup replay against Crystal Palace which had won the boss his first English trophy. Then things started to go wrong.

We carried on winning, but Lee picked up injury after injury and was out of the side a lot. European games seemed to hold a curse as far as he was concerned. During the 1990–91 season when we won the European Cup-Winners' Cup, Lee gave away an own goal when we faced Montpellier in the first leg of the quarter-final at Old Trafford. The strange thing is I cannot remember him doing anything like that in any other competition.

Eventually in January 1994, after just two or three more appearances, he was transferred to Celtic, where Lou Macari had taken over as manager after leaving Stoke.

Galatasaray celebrated as we cursed our luck. We had thrown away a two-goal lead and when we went off at half-time the crowd was pretty restless. They could sense an upset was on the cards and so could we.

Our performance had been poor. The forwards were staying upfield instead of helping to close things down in the middle of the park. Once we had established that early lead we should have made sure that we were solid in defence, but the midfield was being left to fend for itself and there were spaces all over the pitch for the Turks to exploit.

It may have had something to do with the absence of our two regular full-backs Paul Parker and Denis Irwin, but we seemed totally unbalanced. It was our worst defensive performance for ages and we had to save it for the biggest game of the season.

You have to remember that in order to play in the European Cup you have to win your country's championship. You then face other champions at every stage of the competition. It is Europe's top tournament and we were on the verge of throwing away everything we had worked for in the last twelve months.

The boss was as stunned as we were when we got into the dressing-room. He could not believe the way we were defending: 'You are all over the place. You have to get your act together.'

He was remarkably calm in his half-time briefing as he tried to steady a ship that was rapidly taking on water. He told us that our discipline had gone and players were doing things they would not normally risk in an effort to put it right. The harder we were trying the worse it got.

The Turks had the upper hand. They had scored two away goals which would be valuable in the event of a draw, and we had only one option in the second half and that was to go at them and try to win the first leg.

As the second half started we took the game to them, but they held us off. We created a couple of chances but Galatasaray were growing in confidence and their supporters were having a field day in the corner of the main stand. They had a huge drum which beat out the rhythm for their chanting and I think just about every Turkish restaurant owner in England and his staff had taken the night off to be at the game.

In the 63rd minute they went wild when a shot beat big Peter and smacked against a post. The ball rebounded into the path of the oncoming Kubilay and he scored his second of the night. After leading 2–0 we were 3–2 behind.

Now the writing was on the wall. We had to fight back and we were ready to risk everything.

Then the game was disrupted when what appeared to be two Turkish supporters ran on to the pitch. We felt it was an attempt to waste time. They seemed to be carrying a flaming torch and ran from one corner of the ground across towards the half-way line. Play stopped and we could see the police getting ready to move in when big Peter came out of his goal and grabbed one of them.

He wrestled him roughly to the ground, then picked him up, carried him to the side of the pitch and threw him into the advertising hoardings. The police arrested him and by this time had caught his accomplice. Both were led away but vital minutes had been used up and it was unlikely that the referee would allow for all the time that had been wasted.

It turned out that the 'torch' was in fact a Turkish flag which was being burned as a form of protest. Both men were Kurdish students who appeared in court the next day and were fined for trespassing on the pitch – a local bye-law in the Borough of Trafford. They had come up from London to use the game for a political demonstration because it was being screened throughout Europe. They were publicizing their cause and had nothing to do with football.

That was not the way it was seen by the vast television audience and Peter found himself the target of criticism for the way *he* had attacked a fan. I think any one of us would have done the same thing if we could have got hold of one of the demonstrators, but later the implications were pointed out. What might have happened if they had been such fanatics that they had been carrying some kind of weapon? It could have been a dangerous situation although I am convinced that if the intruder had been wielding an axe big Peter would have still gone for him.

Since the incident Steve Bruce has often joked that he is waiting for Peter to do the same sort of thing to him if they have one of their arguments during a game. Both are such perfectionists that if one of them makes a mistake they let the other know, but I hope it never end with Brucie being thrown off the pitch!

Play restarted but we had to find our momentum again. There was a long standing record at stake. Manchester United have never lost a home tie in a European game since they became the first English club to challenge for success on that level during the 1950s. That night, 20 October 1993, we came within nine minutes of ending that run.

Eric Cantona was the saviour when a cross came into a packed Turkish goalmouth at the Stretford End. Somehow he forced the ball home to level the scores, and in the dying minutes we threw everything at Galatasaray to try to snatch victory.

The Turks held out and celebrated in fine style as they left the pitch. They obviously thought the tie was over and that we would stand no chance in Istanbul.

We were sickened yet we felt that we had the ability to beat them in Turkey. We kept telling ourselves that it was down to a single game, that one goal over there could put us through. But the newspapers gave us a slamming the next day. 'No Turkish Delight for the Champions!' Predictable but true.

There was no time for feeling sorry for ourselves, we had to get back to Premiership business.

I was left out for the trip to Goodison Park three days after the European upset as the boss once again changed things. Paul Parker was still missing with flu but Denis Irwin came back as Lee Martin played his last league game for United, and possibly his last in English football.

'Snoz' made up for his nightmare moment against the Turks by laying on the only goal of the game but it was our other Lee who scored. Sharpey ran on to the cross and hit a fierce left-foot volley which gave Neville Southall no chance. It was one of the best goals of the season and it helped us to maintain our lead at the top.

I have no idea what sort of demands were being made on the Turks while we were getting on with things on the domestic front, but I am sure that they did not have to play the same number of games we faced between the two legs. In the 14-day period we played two important league matches plus the next round of the Coca-Cola Cup. In England we take it for granted that successful sides are going to be faced with a game every three or four days, but it is probably asking too much.

Our next cup opponents were Leicester City, who were doing well in Division One and were at the time hotly fancied to win one of the two automatic promotion places. Anyone who claimed that there was little difference between the top sides in the Premiership and their counterparts in the First Division got a sharp shock that night. The gap was there for all to see and I was delighted to be part of the side which helped to illustrate it.

We lined up:

Schmeichel
Phelan Bruce Pallister Martin
McClair Keane Robson
Kanchelskis Hughes Sharpe

No Cantona, no Giggs, no Ince, but we put five goals past Leicester in what was seen as one of our best performances up to that stage of the season. I think it only fair to say that few teams could have lived with us that night.

Steve Bruce reached a career milestone when after 7 minutes in typical style he got on to the end of a Lee Sharpe corner to head the ball out of the reach of Leicester's 'keeper Gavin Ward. It was Steve's 100th career goal and that is a pretty good record for a centre-half.

It opened the floodgates, and before Brucie got his 101st in the 85th minute, Brian McClair, Lee Sharpe and Mark Hughes all scored in a 5–1 win.

In the second half Denis Irwin came on for Gary Pallister who had pulled a muscle trying to make a sprint for goal. The injury was bad news for us as it kept Gary out for the next two games, one of which was the second leg against Galatasaray. Ryan Giggs replaced Lee Sharpe in the 61st minute, but the goal rush had ended and it was Leicester who got some late consolation through a Colin Hill shot, although we felt the goal looked way offside.

It stood, but coming up soon was a disallowed 'goal' which had serious implications for us.

After the Leicester performance the papers were once again full of talk about the championship race being a foregone conclusion. It was flattering to read but we took no notice of what the experts were saying. We knew that one slip and they would be on our backs.

An example of what I mean came on the eve of our next game, the visit of Queen's Park Rangers. They were described by at least one sportswriter as our 'bogey' team. The knockers had reached for the record books and recalled New Year's Day in 1992 when we had lost 4–1 at home to QPR.

Admittedly it was seen by many as the point of the season where we started to let things slip, but it was hardly the start of a downhill slide. Now they were hoping it would happen again but nobody pointed out that since that upset we had played QPR three times, winning once and drawing twice. Hardly a bogey, but you can try to prove anything with statistics.

Eric Cantona and Paul Ince came back for this one and Paul Parker had recovered from his bug and was fit to face his old club. I was out of action after having a minor sinus operation.

The reason was our flight to Turkey the following week, and anyone who has had sinus problems will understand why I needed the treatment before the trip. I had been having severe headaches and pains under my eyes and when the root of the trouble was diagnosed the club surgeon decided to operate, saying it would clear my head and make it easier for me when we flew to Istanbul.

I think that everyone experiences some sort of discomfort when they fly. During take-off and landing the pressure builds up in your head and that is why they always hand out boiled sweets. The swallowing action helps by making your ears 'pop.'

Not for anyone with a sinus problem. We go deaf and dizzy, it feels as if your head is going to explode and it stays with you for a long time after the journey. It is the last thing I wanted before a big game so the operation meant I had to miss the QPR fixture.

We chalked up another win even though the first-half performance was not one of our best. Bradley Allen put Rangers in front when he scored with a header in the 8th minute after Les Ferdinand got his head onto a corner. Ferdie knocked the ball back into our box after it looked as though we had cleared the danger but Allen ran in and caught us napping. Surely all that talk about the QPR bogey was not going to catch up with us?

That was the 10th league goal we had conceded in 13 matches, but on the credit side we chalked up numbers 26 and 27 that afternoon thanks to strikes from Eric Cantona and Mark Hughes. Both our goals came during a four minute spell in the second half and they turned the game round. Even though we only won 2–1 we played some good football in the later stages of the game and should have had more to show for the effort.

On Monday 1 November we got ready for our trip into the unknown. We all gathered at Manchester airport and were given a good send-off by the well-wishers who were around. That is one of the things which has always puzzled me when we flew out to European games. It seems that all the ground staff and anyone else we meet in the airport is a United supporter. But if we happen to come home after an upset it is usually the City fans who check our passports and sort out the luggage! I reckon they wait for the result then volunteer for extra duty.

There was one trip when we were diverted to Speke Airport in Liverpool, and you can imagine the welcome we got there. But when it comes to receptions . . . read on.

The trip to Turkey started perfectly. We had a great flight out and we were all relaxed and confident as we chatted and played cards on the specially-chartered aircraft. There was the usual banter and leg-pulling, a lot of it directed towards the media contingent who were at the back of the plane. We were taking bets on which one of them would be the most legless when we got to Istanbul, and every time we heard the rattle of the drinks trolley the odds altered!

The feeling in the camp and amongst the Press was that we stood a good chance despite the Old Trafford upset. A 1-0 win would take us through, and when you took into account that we had only failed to score in one of the 20 games we had played since the start of the season, we had every reason to believe that we could do it. What did I say about statistics?

When we got to Istanbul things started to change. We arrived to a hostile welcome, with hundreds of supporters crammed into the airport reception area chanting and waving banners. There had been stories about death threats against Peter Schmeichel for the way he had handled the demonstrators at Old Trafford and we almost began to believe them! We had all been told that the Galatasaray followers were fanatics and here was proof.

I suppose it was nothing new to those of us who had played abroad a lot, but some of our younger players looked a bit alarmed. The chanting grew louder as we walked through the airport building to our coach. The Turks pushed forward against a cordon of police and stuck out banners saying 'Welcome to The Hell.' Some accused us of being 'Barbarians' and implied that we would meet a sticky end. Some of the slogans were politically motivated and others told us that we were in for a shock when we got to the Alisamiyen Stadium.

We boarded the coach, leaving the Press to run the gauntlet and the betting was off. As soon as they saw the reception committee everyone of them turned stone-cold sober! We had been warned.

I honestly took no notice because I knew that once we got out on to the pitch it was going to be eleven players against eleven and all the slogans, all the chanting and all the threats in the world could not change that.

Then we were driven away into an entirely different world. We left behind the noise and dust of the airport and were taken to our hotel which was excellent. The service and food were first-class and the Turks went out of their way to make us feel at home. We had a morning of sight-seeing and visited the famous landmarks of Istanbul, then 24 hours before the game were taken to the Alisamiyen for a training session.

We were quite happy with the Galatasaray facilities, which although basic were quite adequate, and it was better than many stadia I have played in. The boss laid out his plans for the next evening when he wanted us to go for that vital goal and keep things tight at the back. We knew that the Turks would defend because they had the away goal advantage but one strike for us could change that.

The game started at 5.30 p.m. English time, meaning that back home many people would be following things on their car radios as they returned from work. Those lucky enough to leave early could catch the game on television.

Lucky? They must have thought they were watching a horror movie.

When we got to the ground there were thousands outside. It was take two of the airport welcome but this time the reception committee was a hundred times bigger.

We took our usual stroll onto the pitch, which we reached after climbing up a steep flight of concrete steps from the underground dressing-room area.

Then the noise hit us. The whole place was packed with 40,000 yelling Turks and it was pretty clear that their message was not 'Welcome to Istanbul.'

Then came the game. There is only one way I can describe what happened. We were robbed!

We thought that we had got off to another perfect start when I slotted a pass through to Lee Sharpe. He raced on to the ball and ran clear of the Turkish defence to fire home a low powerful shot.

Brilliant – and the best way of silencing the crowd, most of whom had been in the stadium for at least four hours before we got there.

But wait! Lee was given offside even though we were convinced that he had timed his run perfectly. It was a real body blow, especially afterwards when television proved that the officials were wrong.

As far as I am concerned the tie was lost at that moment. If we had gone ahead Galatasaray would have been devastated. They would have had to come at us and open up the game. They had taken advantage of our off-night at Old Trafford and we knew that there was no way we were going to play as badly again.

Galatasaray realized we meant to go at them and they defended in depth. If the ball went out of play the ball boys were slow to recover it, everything was being geared to frustrate us and waste as much time as possible.

Both sides went off at half-time still looking for that first break-through. The boss was optimistic and told us that if we could step things up a bit we could still win it. We tried to pressurize them in the second half but they pulled everybody back behind the ball and held out against all we could muster.

The crowd was getting a bit restless the more we went at Galatasaray and when the Turks saw an opening and mounted a rare attack the noise was deafening. At one point the ball ran off the field close to the Galatasaray bench and one of their staff refused to hand it to Eric Cantona who wanted to get on with things. Eric pushed him out of the way and there was an almighty rumpus.

It had quickly become clear to us why the locals call the Alisamiyen 'The Hell.' Well before the kick-off the supporters had been letting off flares which they held above their heads pouring out putrid fumes in huge plumes of coloured smoke. Some of them threw fireworks onto the edge of the pitch during the game, and while it might have looked spectacular at times it was difficult to breath in the choking atmosphere.

We knew that the longer the game went on, it was our chances of getting through which were going up in smoke. Everyone in football is aware that there are times when you need a little more than skill to win games. You need to have luck and that had deserted us.

Galatasaray had got their break when Arif Erdem scored that opening goal for them at Old Trafford. I doubt if he will ever score another goal like that in the rest of his career. It was a one-in-a-thousand shot which came at as decisive a moment for Galatasaray as did our disallowed 'goal' in Istanbul.

One kick, and one decision by the referee which went against us. That is football.

But as far as I am concerned we did not lose the game in Turkey, we lost it at Old Trafford. No side can expect to give away three goals at home after leading 2–0 and still succeed. The Turks were dead and buried and yet they found inspiration from a single goal and fully deserved their draw.

But there is more to this story than that. To quote a well known football blooper: 'There goes the final whistle . . . but this game isn't over yet!'

Referee Kurt Rothlisberger blew for time and the fun and games began. I led the lads into the centre circle to applaud our supporters who had been crammed into one section of the stadium at the opposite end to the players' entrance. We had noticed during the game they had been unusually quiet. We thought it might have had something to do with the result, but discovered later that they had been warned that chanting for the opposition might cause problems amongst the locals!

I noticed that Eric Cantona had gone up to the referee and thought I saw him make a gesture with his finger and thumb as he spoke. It seemed to me that he had formed a circle to tell the Swiss official that his song for Europe was getting 'Zero points' from the French judge!

However there is another version of what happened. The referee claimed that Eric's fingers did not form a circle, but a 'V' sign so he had pulled out his red card. He said later: 'I know exactly what that gesture means and that is why I sent him off.'

Then all hell broke out in The Hell. Eric was furious. I ran across to him to pull him away from the Swiss official who could obviously understand French even though he was from the German-speaking part of his country.

The Turkish fans were running onto the pitch and I took Eric by the arm and led him away, saying: 'Come on, let's get out of this.

Forget about it. The game's over now and there's nothing we can do about it.'

Eric walked with me and I was still holding him by one arm when a Turkish policeman came up and took hold of the other. Eric was still angry and it was obvious that he thought that the referee's decisions had cost us the game, but he was calming down as we pushed our way through the crowd towards the tunnel.

There were no problems, Eric was between the two of us walking slowly and saying nothing. He seemed to have cooled down totally by the time we reached the top of the steps. When we got there about twenty or thirty policemen with riot shields were gathered round the exit. Some faced inward, others had their backs to us and were watching the Turkish fans who were swarming on to the running track as they tried to mob the Galatasaray players.

I paused to let Eric go down the steps first and turned to thank the policeman for helping us when suddenly he swung a punch. He hit Eric fully on the back of the head. It was not just a slap but a full-blooded blow and it knocked him stumbling forward down the concrete steps.

He grabbed at the handrail to regain his balance and prevented himself falling several feet. Then he turned to see what had happened as I swung round to try to grab the policeman.

His colleagues waded in and I was hit with a shield. It gashed my hand and I was pushed backwards down the steps. The rest of the lads were coming up behind us and saw what happened so they piled in to help and it turned into a bit of a mêlée.

It was all over in a few seconds and was a little one-sided. The police were armed with batons and protected by padded clothing and their shields and helmets. Some of the lads took a few whacks.

I was furious. I thought that it was an absolute outrage, but the policeman who had started it all disappeared into the ruck and was obviously going to get away with it. He had punched a player and created a situation that could quite easily have led to someone being seriously hurt – the police carry guns as well as batons – and yet he managed to escape scot-free.

There was no reason for the punch and I wonder what it would have been like if things had been the other way round. If Eric had struck him, he would probably still be in a Turkish jail.

I know he may have a reputation of being quick-tempered but Eric Cantona is not a villain. The trouble is he is a man who speaks his mind. He is a perfectionist and feels that if someone does something he disagrees with he is entitled to give his opinion. This has got him into trouble with the footballing authorities who prefer players to be seen and not heard.

During a game he is often the target of opponents' crafty digs and kicks when the referee is not looking, but he will retaliate openly because he feels he has the right. Eric is rarely, if ever, the one who makes the first aggresive move. One of his favourite expressions is: 'Football is a game not a war.'

But that night in Istanbul it seemed more like a battlefield as we fought our way off the pitch. When we got to the dressing-room the boss had the door locked behind us and we could hear all the rumpus going on outside as the police poured down the steps and packed the corridors.

We sat in our dungeon as the people from the media joined in the pushing and shoving. Television cameras, tape recorders, flash guns and a sea of bodies crammed the doorway as we changed in silence.

Some time between his dispute with the referee and our reaching the sanctuary of the dressing-room, Eric had been stopped by a French journalist from L'Equipe, his country's top sporting magazine. They know each other quite well and Eric was asked what had been going on. His response landed him in deep trouble.

There happened to be a television crew on hand and they stuck a microphone under his nose and broadcast what he was saying to the French reporter. Whether Eric meant his words to be used as a direct quote only he knows, but he touched a nerve in a highly sensitive area.

During the summer there had been a major uproar in France when their champions Marseille were involved in a bribery scandal which led to them being kicked out of the European Cup. This must have been in Eric's mind when he said something along the lines of: 'There have been many stories that referees in Europe can be bought and when you see a display like the one we have witnessed tonight it makes you wonder.'

Next day the story hit the English newspapers and the balloon went up. It was a mistake. If what Eric was supposed to have said was true he was sure to land himself in trouble with UEFA.

Understandably referee Rothlisberger hit back: 'Throughout my life I have stood for fair play and the standards of a gentleman. Nobody would dream of trying to buy me – they know what my answer would be. At the end of the game Cantona came up to me and made a rude gesture with two fingers and said 'Thank you'. I am fully aware what that gesture means and I showed him the red card. Technically, under the rules, I may not have been correct in doing that but psychologically I did the right thing.'

The Cantona incident had taken the spotlight away from the attack on us by the police and that angered me. Can you imagine what sort of uproar there would have been had an English policeman struck a Galatasaray player at Old Trafford? We would never have heard the end of it. Manchester United would have been banned from Europe, and probably so too would the rest of the English clubs.

Yet the Turks went virtually unpunished. They were later fined a few thousand pounds for setting off fireworks and allowing their supporters to encroach on the pitch, but United were also made to pay for the so-called indiscipline of the players and letting those two demonstrators run on to the pitch at Old Trafford.

I could not believe my eyes when I read some time later that Rene Eberle, who is the head of UEFA's disciplinary committee, had refused to believe our version of what had happened in Istanbul even though I am positive that there must have been television evidence to back up our claims about the clash with the police.

'You give me proof of what happened between the police and players and I will give you the opposite,' is what Mr Eberle is reported to have said. He did add that the sending off would not appear on Eric's record because the referee was wrong to produce the red card after the final whistle, but Eric would be punished for his after-match comments.

It has been argued that television is not going to be used to decide issues during a game but it seems that it is all right to use it to condemn a player even when the camera crew appeared to be eavesdropping. There were stories that Eric might face a long ban and that the UEFA verdict might even affect his United career.

The papers were full of speculation that he could walk out of English football and take his skills elsewhere, but that was probably wishful thinking on behalf of the anti-United brigade. Some said he would pack in the game completely if the UEFA punishment was severe.

The case of Georgy Donkov of Bulgaria was quoted. He had been banned from international football for five years for spitting at a referee and linesman but there was hardly a comparison. It was another example of sensationalism from the tabloids.

The club tried to put things in perspective and issued a statement distancing itself from anything which might or might not have been said. It said it was far from convinced that Eric had been quoted correctly, but added: 'Manchester United want to make it clear that we are happy with the referee's integrity and that there is no evidence of any impropriety. He handled the game fairly and properly. '

Eric was banned for four European games – two two-legged ties – but he was allowed to continue playing for France in their World Cup qualifying games and the UEFA decision had no effect on English domestic games.

If Eric committed a footballing crime I still think the Turks got away with murder. I am not saying Galatasaray should have been kicked out of the competition because we were attacked by the police, but I think that there was a strong case to answer for some action to be taken along those lines when we heard what happened to our supporters, when a third issue sprang to light.

It involved a party of United fans who were staying at the Tansa Hotel in Istanbul and eventually led to action being taken by the British government. On the morning of the game the British consul in Istanbul had issued a statement that a group of our supporters had been arrested for wrecking their hotel. We heard the story as we watched breakfast television and we were all worried that it might lead to some sort of punishment being meted out against the club. Following the Heysel Stadium incident and the five-year ban on English clubs things have been very sensitive.

Because of this United has tried to encourage supporters to travel to European games in groups officially organized by the club's Membership Scheme. They realize that it is impossible to stop anyone going anywhere if they decide that they want to make their own arrangements, but tickets for major games are only sold to registered supporters who have joined the scheme.

We knew that the club parties were not flying into Istanbul until that lunchtime and suspected that a group of troublemakers who had travelled to Istanbul without tickets might be at the root of things. How wrong we were and I apologize for having any such thoughts.

When the truth emerged it appeared that our supporters were subjected to atrocious treatment and a lot of innocent people were branded criminals in the eyes of the Turks. Apparently it all began the night before our game when there was some sort of an argument in a bar where the customers were watching a European match on television. It involved one of Istanbul's other clubs but most of the Turks in the bar were Galatasaray fans.

When the opposition scored the handful of United fans cheered. The Turks did not like this. Afterwards they followed the English fans back to their hotel and attacked them. Windows were broken and during a long siege they even drove a vehicle at the doors.

The police were called and all the United supporters were arrested. The majority of them had been nowhere near the original incident, yet they were dragged from their beds as they slept and hauled off in police vans. They were held in the cells, men and women alike, and at least one of them was a 70-year-old pensioner, and the next day were sent home after having 'deportee' stamped on their passports. None of them saw the game.

Others who were alleged to have been the culprits who had sparked off the incident and included the tour organizer who had not been in the bar, were held in jail for weeks as they faced trial and possible prison sentences.

Back home this brought all sorts of reactions. Questions were asked in the House of Commons and an all-party group of MPs raised support on their behalf, collecting evidence from the innocent 'deportees' who told of the horrors they had been subjected to.

When eventually the trial was held they were cleared of all charges and sent home, but when they announced their demands for compensation against the Turkish authorities they were retried in their absence and found guilty!

Eventually the Home Office arranged for new passports to be issued removing the deportee stain which could have affected them if they took any future trips abroad. Relations between Britain and Turkey were a little strained for a while.

It had also emerged that some supporters on the official trips had problems too. Many of our fans went all the way to Turkey having bought tickets for the game in advance, and were not allowed into the stadium because their seats had been reallocated to the locals. They were told that they had not got to the ground early enough, even though it was still an hour away from kick-off time.

Then as they left the stadium the groups travelling with the club's flights were attacked by Turkish fans. They were forced to make the journey back to the airport lying on the floors of their buses as stones smashed through the windows and rained in on them. They were the lucky ones.

We have to ask the question: would an English club have been allowed to continue in the competition if visiting supporters had been forced to endure the same treatment? During the weeks after our exit the row continued, but Galatasaray went on to play in the European Champions League. Nothing could change that.

Our exit was the biggest blow we had taken since we missed out on the title in 1992. We knew that the only way we could recover was to win the championship again and qualify for the Champions' Cup in 1994–95.

I realized that I would not be part of that campaign and it made it all the harder to take. I had ended my last European match having a punch-up with a Turkish copper!

I have got to make it clear that I mean no discredit to Galatasaray, and do not want it to sound like sour grapes because we had been knocked out. As far as their players are concerned they beat us fair and square, but I feel that UEFA still has a long way to go to ensure the safety of supporters travelling to games in places like Turkey, and if this cannot be done then those countries should not be allowed to enter the competitions.

If there were similar incidents in England you could guarantee that UEFA would throw the book at the club involved, and as we flew home from Istanbul immediately after the game we all wondered what might have happened to us if we had won! It was pretty rough being a loser over there, but if we had knocked out the home side it would have been World War Three.

We had to put the disappointment of Turkey behind us and get our act together for the next game. The fixture compilers had given us the perfect tonic after a European upset – we were flying home to get ready for the Manchester derby at Maine Road.

This was going to be a stiff test, even though we knew that the boss would make changes from the side which had played in Turkey. Mark Hughes and Andrei Kanchelskis were brought back as Gary Pallister returned from his injury.

When we got to Maine Road for the Sunday televised game I have to admit that quite a few of us were surprised to discover that so many of the City fans were Galatasaray supporters. Quite a few of them had Turkish flags and chanted their name.

It was amazing how they had switched allegiance. I thought that they supported Atletico Madrid . . . or was that only because they knocked us out of the Cup-Winners' Cup in 1991?

I was on the bench to witness what I thought was a fantastic achievement by the lads, although at one point I have to admit that it looked as if City were going to upset the form book. At half-time they led 2–0 thanks to two goals from big Niall Quinn and we seemed to be paying the price for all the travelling and disappointments of the week.

But we staged an incredible come-back and raised our game after the break. It was great to watch as Eric showed that his Turkish experiences had been quickly forgotten. He latched on to a mistake by Michel Vonk, City's Dutch defender, who thought he could reach Tony Coton with his back pass. Eric slipped in and knocked the ball home.

That was all we needed. Spirits were raised and we had got ourselves back in the game after only 7 minutes of the second half. We tried to crack the City defence but somehow they held out until, with 12 minutes left, Eric scored again. It was just after Ryan Giggs had been brought on as substitute to replace Andrei, and from almost his first touch Giggsy helped to create goal number two as he slipped the ball through to Eric. We were level.

Many sides would have settled for that but this was the Manchester derby and a lot of pride was at stake. We could see City were rocking. They had been in front for 78 minutes and now we had them going backwards.

With 3 minutes left Denis Irwin went on a run down the left flank. Lee Sharpe back-heeled the ball through Richard Edghill's legs, Denis crossed into the box, Sparky went for it but failed to make contact, and Roy Keane, who was coming in fast, ran it into the City net.

Those Galatasaray supporters were stunned. I suppose it is only natural that fans will look for a way of taunting the opposition, and City's supporters were not the only ones to remind us of our Turkish nightmare in the weeks to come.

We had been to The Hell and come back to win at Maine Road and as far as Manchester United was concerned that was the best possible way of showing that we were far from finished. It was early November, we were top of the table, 11 points clear of Norwich and Aston Villa, and 14 ahead of Blackburn who were lying 8th.

I could tell that it was going to be harder for me to hold my place in midfield because of the way Roy Keane was playing, even though there had been a lot of newspaper talk that I might even get recalled into the England squad. Robson, Waddle and Beardsley were names being mentioned, but not by the man who mattered.

But my manager told me that I was playing in the next game . . . and I knew why. We were due to face Wimbledon at Old Trafford.

CHAPTER FOUR

Into '94 – The Race Is On

A THIRD OF THE SEASON HAD GONE AND WE STILL LED THE Premiership. We were disappointed not to have done better in the European Cup but we knew that being out of that competition meant we could turn our attention towards domestic achievement.

In the tabloids they were playing a guessing game. Could anyone challenge Manchester United? If so, who? Norwich, Aston Villa, Leeds were all possible contenders. We were sitting on an 11-point lead with Norwich and Aston Villa the closest to us. They were followed by Leeds, Liverpool, Arsenal and Queen's Park Rangers who each had 14 points less than us. We knew that there were still 28 games to play so the race was hardly over, but we were stretching the field and determined to keep up the pace.

The pundits predicted that if we could get through the Christmas holiday period and maintain our comfortable lead, we were home and dry.

The feeling in the dressing-room was one of confidence but not complacency. We knew of the pitfalls that a season can hold, and while Christmas was acoming we were fully aware that it might just be the time when we might slip and let somebody get on our tails.

Christmas has proved to be a make or break time for many teams. Although it was still five weeks away we knew that we had to prepare for one of football's busy periods when games are crammed into the holiday period. At such times squads can be weakened by injuries, with no time to recover, and the heavier pitches take their toll.

Ironically there was a hint of Christmas in the air the day Wimbledon came to Old Trafford. The 'United Review,' our match programme, was full of suggestions for presents, and as I sat in the players' lounge flicking through its pages following my pre-match meal there was every reason to believe that somebody was having an early party in the next room.

It was The Dons and their famous ghetto blaster, which was rattling the tiles of their dressing-room as I tried to relax. They really are a barmy lot, but I have to confess that I have a bit of a soft spot for Wimbledon – and I don't mean the nearest patch of quicksand.

I have come to admire the way that they have been able to survive in the top section of our game on a shoestring budget, yet without the slightest hint of any problems. They live off gates of three to five thousand, which can hardly pay the players' wages, yet year in year out they always seem to disrupt the plans of the big boys.

Add to this the fact that they have never really faced the threat of relegation since they came through from nowhere and reached the First Division, and you can see what a remarkable club it is.

They have earned their nickname of the 'party poopers' because they have a great knack of being able to ruin a reputation. If they can stop one of the glamour clubs from winning something Wimbledon are in their element.

Nowadays they are not quite the headache they proved to be when they first joined the élite. Then they were just a bunch of thugs . . . and were proud of the fact!

As far as I am concerned the way they went about things in those days was not good for football but thankfully over the years they have changed and have certainly won my respect.

What is also incredible about the club is they seem to have created an endless flow of talent from lower or non-league clubs. They must have a good scouting system, coupled with a backroom staff which has the ability to bring players through. They must be able to see in them things that other clubs have missed, then they bring them into their system and transform them into quality players who perform well in the Premier League. If the player doesn't stay with Wimbledon he is sold on at a vast profit. All that happens next is rather than leaving a gap in their side they go back to their stockpile and start over again.

Wimbledon have changed their style of play considerably in recent years, but are still inclined to hit the long free kick into the danger zone, or drop huge throw-ins into your penalty area for big John Fashanu to get on the end of. They can play some orthodox attractive football and have developed from the ugly ducklings of the league into challenging, more acceptable opponents.

I knew I stood a good chance of playing against them because this always seemed to be one of the games when the boss would include me in his plans. He knew that I would not be intimidated by them, and that I had no problems as far as the physical stuff was concerned. I have heard that Wimbledon can be physical from time to time!

I also got my chance for the Old Trafford game because Roy Keane was injured, but I was glad to be back in the middle of things after being forced to watch the derby from the bench.

I knew we would be treating them with added respect as I read through the programme notes and discovered it had been a year since we had last been beaten at Old Trafford. No prizes for guessing who did the damage that day. Yes, it was Wimbledon. We went down 1–0 but took our revenge in the closing game of the 1992–93 season when we faced them at Selhurst Park in our first real outing as champions.

Twenty-three games later we chalked up another win, thanks to goals from Gary Pallister, Mark Hughes and Andrei Kanchelskis, although once again John Fashanu gave us a shock when he popped up with an equalizer. Fash got his head to a useful cross from full-back Warren Barton and rubbed out Pally's only goal of the season.

John Fashanu is a talented player who has made headline news many times and often for the wrong reasons. He is a big man and it is obvious he can look after himself. Four days after we had beaten The Dons, he was to find himself at the centre of another controversy when he was involved in an incident with Gary Mabbutt of Tottenham.

Gary was left with serious facial injuries after a collision with Fash. Allegations were made that Gary had been elbowed and it was not the first time that a Wimbledon player had found himself in the thick of things. Eventually the Football Association decided there was no case to answer, with no obvious intent in the challenge, but it sparked off a campaign from the Professional Footballers' Association to outlaw illegal use of the elbow.

I have often been asked what it is like to play against Wimbledon and the most notorious member of the famous Crazy Gang, Vinny Jones. Vinny has quite a reputation as some sort of hard case, but you might be surprised to discover that I think he is a smashing lad.

Off the pitch he is a larger-than-life character and is terrific company. On the field it can be a different story and we all know that he sometimes gets a rush of blood and does something rash. Unfortunately he has injured one or two players during his career and only he knows how many of those incidents have been intentional. This will always be held against him, but as far as I am concerned he has never been a problem.

One part of the Wimbledon approach is to try wind up the opposition. They use a lot of banter and gamesmanship on the field doing what cricketers would call 'sledging.' But that sort of thing has been going on in football since the game began, and although Vinny is supposed to be top man when it comes to the wind-up he had never said one thing to me during a game.

I have overheard some of the comments he has made in the direction of other players, not very much of which would be considered printable, but I think that he realizes it would be water off a duck's back if he used me as his target.

If you show you can be intimidated by someone they will go out of their way to make things worse for you. I have no doubt at all that some of Wimbledon's success has hinged on this intimidation factor. The United side which faced them when they first came into the First Division was one of their victims but there is no way that they could do the same sort of thing to the Manchester United of today.

We cruised to an easy win which was our thirteenth Premiership victory of the season, and it came on an afternoon when Blackburn Rovers also won at Ewood Park. They overcame Southampton to take their points total to 26. We were 14 points in front of them but Rovers were about to set off on a remarkable run and emerge as our main rivals.

We ignored all the predictions that we would walk away with the title before Easter. We also took no notice of news that the bookmakers were about to stop betting on our retaining the title. We were confident in our own ability but we knew that we were not infallible.

Our pride took a dent when Ipswich came to Old Trafford for our next Premiership game. Our thoughts were elsewhere before the kick-off because we all realized whom we might have been playing had we got through in the Champions' Cup against Galatasaray. Instead of Ipswich we would have been hosts to Barcelona. That Turkish nightmare would haunt us for a while.

We got a sharp reminder of what might have been when we watched the opening stages of Norwich's UEFA tie against Inter-Milan which was being shown on television in the players' lounge as we prepared for action. Barcelona at Old Trafford would have been fantastic.

Instead we had to settle for Ipswich and a game that was anything but a thriller. It was a sign of things to come as word spread on the football grapevine that someone had found out how to contain us.

Don't get me wrong, Ipswich had hardly discovered our Achilles heel. Teams have tried what they did before but they performed a thorough containing job and confronted us with a system which was to be copied time and again during the remainder of the season. Simply, they tried not to be beaten even if it meant sacrificing their own chances of winning.

If that sounds strange it means that they concentrated on defence, made sure that they kept their shape, and left us with few openings. As for scoring themselves, I suppose they would have taken a chance if it had come along but they seemed quite happy to soak up all we had to offer.

I have often listened to people who feel that a points-for-goals system should be introduced into our game, and while I am not in favour its supporters might have won a few votes at Old Trafford that night. Ipswich played with five across the back and pulled their two strikers into wide positions, meaning another five players spread across midfield. This left Steve Bruce and Gary Pallister with a lot of possession in our back four, but they had nobody to play the ball to because everyone was well covered by a solid marking system.

Our only chance of success hinged on us being able to crack the system and score. If that had happened their plan would have fallen down and they would have had to adjust things and try for an equalizer.

It was a tactical battle and Ipswich won it 0–0!

The longer the game went on the more frustrated our supporters became, and anxiety set in amongst the lads. I knew just how a boxer feels when his opponent back-pedals away from him as he tries to make a fight of it. Ipswich kept retreating behind the ball, and even though we chased them we were unable to land a knock-out punch.

During the rest of the season the Mick McGiven system was adapted to suit other sides, and in the end the Old Trafford fans got used to seeing such games.

Did it pay off for Ipswich in the long run? By the end of the season they had drawn 16 of their Premiership games but their ploy almost backfired. Since the introduction of the 3 points-for-a-win policy, not losing has become less valuable than a win-lose-win situation. Ten draws produces 10 points, but 5 wins and 5 defeats brings 15. Ipswich were lucky to escape relegation . . . although in the end they managed to stay up thanks to a draw!

However, it was the supporters I felt sorry for that night. They had paid good money to see a game but it was as exciting as watching paint dry. It wasn't only the United followers who had my sympathy but those fans who had travelled all the way from Suffolk to sit through 90 minutes of negative football on a freezing Manchester night. I don't think Ipswich had one single shot on goal, although while being critical of this approach I am not blaming anyone for trying to outfox us.

The challenge for any side is to try to beat the opposition, and I suppose that if you feel you are not good enough to win then the next best thing is not to lose. That, though, is not my style, nor will it ever be the way they play at Manchester United.

The Ipswich result sparked off more debate on the sports pages, 'United are vulnerable after all', but it was not the main headline stealer. That went to the demise of England under the management of Graham Taylor.

During the period between our win at Maine Road and that draw against Ipswich, England had been knocked out of the World Cup and this led to the much-speculated resignation of Taylor.

So started another guessing game. Who would be the next England boss?

I was flattered to find myself being put forward as a likely candidate, and I have to admit that I have never hidden the fact that I had ambitions in that direction. But when I discovered that the press conference which followed the Ipswich game was being directed more towards that subject than the game we had just played, I did a neat body swerve. I felt it was all a little premature.

At that time the FA had made no approaches to me and all the names being put forward were pure speculation. Ron Atkinson, Bobby Robson, Terry Venables, Trevor Francis and many others were simply guesses by the media, and I have often thought that the papers do this to cover themselves for the day when the news is announced. Then they can claim to have told their readers first. I made it clear that I did not know how I would react if any offer came from the FA . I said I would keep an open mind.

In truth, at the time I was only interested in playing for Manchester United and seeing what we could achieve during the remainder of the season. I had not given up hope of continuing with United for another season, or if this was not possible of playing elsewhere during 1994–95.

It would take me past my thirty-eighth birthday, but provided I felt as fit as I did at that moment, I could see no reason to retire as a player.

The next game for us was the trip to Coventry, and because I was having treatment for a slight hamstring strain, the boss brought his son Darren into the side. It was his first, and last, Premiership start of the season. Darren was feeling unsettled and had asked his father to make him available for transfer. A few weeks into the New Year he was sold to Wolves where eventually Graham Taylor became his manager. Small world, isn't it?

It must have been difficult for Darren while he was at Old Trafford even though he never showed it. He was treated no differently to any other player either by the lads or by the manager. When he was emerging as a young player Alex had been torn between letting him go to another club – Brian Clough wanted to take him on at Nottingham Forest – or signing him for United. He took the advice of those around him and Darren progressed through the club's youth system to become a useful midfielder.

When a boy is developing as a player no-one really knows how he will turn out and Alex could have been in an embarrassing position if he had let Darren sign for another club, then found himself wanting to buy him for United. Perhaps one day my son Ben will give me the same sort of headache. I can only hope.

For a second successive season we beat Coventry 1–0 and this was another dour game, although it was not quite in the same category as the Ipswich match. Denis Irwin, who scored the winner on our previous visit to Highfield Road, played a leading part this time too. He and Ryan Giggs combined well down the left flank, and when the cross came in Eric Cantona was there to direct a close-range header beyond Steve Ogrizovic. The big goalkeeper had been busy during the first hour and had pulled off some good saves but he was finally thwarted.

Coventry is a hard place to go. They are a difficult side to beat and they have some very skilful players but we took maximum points and we could see a pattern emerging. At home we would find ourselves facing opponents who more often than not adopted a defensive pattern, but in front of their own supporters sides had to open out. With our speed and the variations of attack we stood a better chance of winning away from Old Trafford than we did in front of our own spectators!

Proof of this was that, out of the 8 away games we had played up to that stage, we had won seven; while at home two of our nine league games had been drawn. A third would follow a week after that win at Coventry.

In between we were back at Goodison Park for the Coca-Cola Cup and found ourselves playing a leading role in the demise of Howard Kendall. I was back in the side after responding to treatment but Roy Keane was still out with the injury he had picked up in the Manchester derby.

We won 2–0 but it could so easily have been more. On a night when we played some lovely passing football the Everton fans showed just how fickle supporters can be.

When Howard returned to Everton after his time in Spain and at Maine Road, they saw him as the Messiah. He would lead them back to the top after his successful time at the club in the early eighties.

Everton were struggling in the League, the club was in the middle of a take-over battle, and the supporters were restless. No sooner had we gone in front, when Mark Hughes chipped a super goal over Neville Southall, than I could hear the crowd turning on their manager.

We created most of the chances as Howard did his best to counteract our efforts by changing tactics. After Ryan Giggs had given us another goal straight after the break he threw on his substitutes Preki and Barlow. But there was nothing he could do to stop us winning.

The gaffer had been quoted in that morning's papers saying he felt Peter Schmeichel had been playing at his peak in the last few games: 'I sense he is going through a mean streak at present. When he is in that kind of form he is the best there is.' He was right and Peter kept his third consecutive clean sheet, showing his special ability in the 53rd minute when Everton were awarded a penalty.

We were 2–0 up and it was a crucial moment as Tony Cottee stepped up to take the spot kick. If he had scored Everton would have been back in the game and might have salvaged something. He hit a hard low shot to Peter's right, but the big Dane was watching like a hawk. He anticipated well, dived low and pulled off a great save.

After that we had two 'goals' disallowed and went through to the fifth round. Howard Kendall lost his job a short while later.

With the European upset now forgotten we were going well on both fronts and there was every reason to believe that we could win at least one trophy, and possibly two. Our position in the League made us clear favourites, although that Blackburn challenge was about to emerge, and we were two rounds away from Wembley in the Coca-Cola Cup.

Blackburn had stuttered slightly before mounting their surge when they lost away to Ipswich. They were then knocked out of the Coca-Cola Cup by Tottenham, reminding us of the pattern of the two previous championships when the winners had made early exits from the domestic knock-outs. Would this help Rovers?

They set off on a run of three successive victories by beating Chelsea 2–0 at Ewood Park. A day earlier we played Norwich at Old Trafford and Mike Walker – who would shortly replace Howard Kendall at Everton – had another attempt at outwitting the gaffer.

In the season's opening game, Norwich had fallen into the trap of trying to defend against us in numbers in a similar way to Ipswich. Unlike their neighbours they left openings probably because it was not the way they usually played.

The Norwich approach has always been open attacking football and they reverted to that at Old Trafford. It was more like the old Norwich. They went for our throats, in a footballing sense.

It was a surprise because we expected the opposite and they caused us all sorts of problems with the best display of attacking football from the opposition that we saw at Old Trafford all season. They had won themselves plenty of friends with their performances in the UEFA Cup, beating Vitesse Arnhem and Bayern Munich, and were due to fly out to Milan, for the second leg of their tie with Inter two days after facing us. We told their players after the game that if they took the same approach in Italy they were in with a chance.

We scored first when Ryan Giggs fired in a shot from a Cantona cross, but Chris Sutton showed why everybody rated him so highly by equalizing within a minute. Brian McClair gave us the lead again just before half-time jumping in to volley as Eric headed down a cross from Denis Irwin.

Were Norwich finished? Not likely, they kept going and got a penalty when Daryl Sutch was brought down by Gary Pallister.

Ruel Fox tucked it away with just two minutes of the second half gone.

We found that it was our turn to defend and they were unlucky not to leave Old Trafford with more than the one point. Unfortunately they couldn't do the same in Italy and lost 1–0 in Milan, going out 2–0 on aggregate.

The pattern of home draw, away win was repeated when we went to Sheffield to take on United at Bramall Lane. No easy game but we won easily.

With Dave Bassett's influence Sheffield have a bit of a Wimbledon approach at set-pieces and use their height and strength to upset the opposition. We knew what to expect but turned on a display of good football that had The Blades well and truly blunted.

We organized ourselves to deal with those problems from free kicks and corners and made sure that we closed down every area around our goal so that they could create nothing. Then we opened out and hit them with the speed of Ryan Giggs and Lee Sharpe, and even though we scored three times through Mark Hughes, Sharpey and Eric Cantona, we could easily have won by four or five. We were top of the table, 15 points clear with 19 games behind us.

Blackburn added to their win over Chelsea by beating Oldham 2–1 at Boundary Park as we drew at Newcastle and we were on a collision course, with Rovers due to face us at Old Trafford on Boxing Day.

Between them Mark Hughes and Eric Cantona had scored 21 goals at this stage of the season. Mark with his robust style was playing the best football I had seen him produce, while Eric was simply being Eric! Since his arrival at Old Trafford the Frenchman has shown his value to the club. His influence has been vital to our success and yet he has been a constant target of the critics.

Before our story of the season ends he will come under some seriously heavy bombardment, but I feel I have to offer something in his defence. Numerous people, some of them ex-players, have criticised his work-rate claiming he doesn't always give 100 per cent. Nonsense.

There are many aspects of Eric's game. He is a highly skilled player who can read a game of football like a navigator follows a complicated map. Whenever he receives the ball he will always try to improve a situation, either by taking on an opponent or by passing to a colleague who is in a more advantageous position. Eric will work hard if the ball is there to be won, and if he has to chase an opponent to retrieve possession he will, but only if he feels it is totally necessary.

I have studied many top-class forwards who do exactly the same. Rather than wearing himself out with senseless chasing he will ration his movement. You will see him weighing up a situation and if he feels there are enough people behind the ball he will take a short breather. It is one of the secrets to his success.

When the ball is released in his direction he is always fresh and ready to create another attack. It is one of the reasons why his passing is so accurate, a tired player makes tired movements and mistakes. The Cantona philosophy is to spread his effort over the whole 90 minutes and keep himself as fresh as he can for the part of the game at which he excels.

I read one article which said that with Eric in our side we were actually playing with ten men. I found it unbelieveable.

It inferred that all the work was being done by the ten and that Eric was being carried along. Are you telling me that ten top-level professional footballers would stand for that? If they thought one player could get away with it they would all do it!

But seriously, we are a team and we all work together. During a game a player has to use his individual skills, that is obvious. But he is also part of a unit and its success depends on each player working for the others.

Eric Cantona can be held up as the perfect example of this. He has great personal talent which he uses to its full, but he also has the ability to assess a situation and create opportunities for others. If a scoring chance comes his way he will seize it, but if he feels that he can create an opening for someone else who is better placed, then that is what he does.

Nobody expects Eric to chase around the field like an excitable terrier that has just been released from its leash, we know that is not his style. As for him being a luxury-class passenger, all I can say is that anyone who plays in the same side as Eric Cantona knows he is a valuable asset and there is no-one at United who would argue otherwise.

Injury had kept me out of the Norwich and Sheffield United games, and I was also out for the next three fixtures which was a bit of a disappointment.

From the wings it was interesting to observe the reaction to our success. Our critics were waiting like a pack of wolves for us to slip, so they could pounce. There were those who said we would not be able to stay the pace and would fall after Christmas in the way we had once thrown away a big lead in the days of Ron Atkinson.

I knew that would not happen because we had two things on our side. We had the experience gained through the two previous campaigns in which we had proved ourselves to be the top team in the country, and we also had the depth of strength in our squad. The boss has bought well, and we have also produced a crop of youngsters who I am convinced will all make it to the top.

Another ridiculous argument put forward as the reason we looked so good was that the rest of the teams in the Premiership were rubbish! What a coincidence it would have been if suddenly during the 1993–94 season 21 clubs found themselves going through a bad patch while one sailed along merrily. Such remarks are both an insult to us and to the rest of the league.

We went into the game at Newcastle with a 15-point lead over Blackburn and saw it cut to 13 by the end of the afternoon. The game ended 1–1 as once again we upset the predicitons that St James's Park might be the place for us to stumble.

As expected it was all high passion and breakneck football with Newcastle throwing everything at us, and if they are supposed to be one of those inferior sides I mentioned a moment ago, tell that to anyone who was at St James's Park that afternoon . . . and to Kevin Keegan.

What they did prove is that they are going to be challenging everybody for honours now they are back in the top section, and their success has been a great boost for Tyneside. My old England team-mate Peter Beardsley had a terrific game and showed the kind of form which was to see him recalled at international level.

Early on Newcastle created quite a few chances. They were on a bit of a run after winning five out of their previous six games, three of them at home. In those they had scored eleven times without conceding a goal so we knew we were in for a battle.

The crowd was tremendous but we choked back a few thousand Geordie cheers when Paul Ince put us in front in the second half and the voices of our supporters broke through. An hour had gone, with both goalkeepers tested several times, when Andrei Kanchelskis went forward on one of his formidable runs. His cross came over, Ryan Giggs got his head to it and Incey finished off with a low, mean-looking shot under Mike Hooper.

The Toon Army might have been silenced for a moment but Newcastle were roused and came at us with all guns firing and predictably it was Andy Cole who got the equalizer. Robert Lee crossed, we left a gap at the near post for Cole to get in and he headed his 22nd goal in all competitions to date. That was formidable form and it continued till the end of the season.

The goal helped to make the last 20 minutes pretty exciting and those claims about other sides being inferior seem all the more ridiculous.

We prepared for the Christmas games with a home clash with Ron Atkinson's Aston Villa, who had surprisingly slipped down the table. When they came to Old Trafford they were 9th and 18 points behind us.

It was a Sunday televised fixture and the previous day Blackburn had beaten Manchester City at Ewood Park. They were in third place, a point behind Leeds but with a game in hand. To add a bit more spice to things our next two home games were against Rovers then Leeds.

The calculators were out. Someone came up with the theory that if we lost to Villa, and Blackburn and Leeds also beat us, we could be caught. Blackburn had a home clash with Everton and a trip to Villa Park after coming to Old Trafford, while Leeds were away to Newcastle and at home to QPR before they faced us.

If one of them had a winning streak . . . if. If my uncle had been a woman he would have been my aunt!

All those theories went out of the window when we beat Villa 3–1 with a flurry of late goals. Eric put us ahead in the 21st minute with a close-range shot from a Roy Keane cross which had Shaun Teale and Earle Barrett in a tangle, but there was a long wait for number two.

It came in the 88th minute when Eric scored his second, beating two former United players en route. First he ran around Paul McGrath, our one-time centre-half, before slotting his shot beyond the reach of Mark Bosnich, who had played a couple of games for us before opting to join Big Ron.

A minute later Mark was fishing the ball out of his net again, this time after Paul Ince had scored. Then just before the final whistle Villa got a bit of consolation when Neil Cox got behind our defence straight from the restart.

Christmas Day came and went in the usual way for professional footballers. We had to train because there was a game the next day and it was the big one. The match the armchair supporters had been waiting for. The Rovers' return.

Blackburn came to Old Trafford looking to avenge that end-of-season defeat on their previous visit. They set out to restrict our movement, and got a great break when Kevin Gallacher forced his way past both Steve Bruce and Gary Pallister. He chipped his shot wide of Peter Schmeichel and we were one down. It was take two of May 1993 when Kevin also scored the opening goal.

We knew that we had a fight on our hands and as I watched the game from the comfort of one of the private boxes which surround Old Trafford I was punching holes in my pockets in frustration. Time and again we got through but could not get the equalizer. Was there a shock on the cards?

I looked at my watch. There were two minutes left and we had been pressurizing constantly. We broke in on the Blackburn right and the ball came off a challenge from Colin Hendry and went out for a corner. He argued that the ball hadn't gone over the line but the linesman and referee disagreed and nothing could change their decision.

I noticed Big Peter Schmeichel was running downfield. He has done it before and was off to play as an added striker. His theory is that if you look as though you are going to lose you might as well gamble on getting an equalizer. If it goes wrong and the opposition break away and score, well you were losing anyway.

Call it Danish logic, but it worked this time. Lee Sharpe took the corner and Peter leapt up in the box together with Gary Pallister and Steve Bruce. All our big guns were up there, and with six feet four of goalkeeper included I mean *all*.

The ball came down into the path of Paul Ince and he rammed it into the back of the net. It was no more than we deserved because Blackburn had not really tried to add to their lead. They got their break and had sat back hoping to hold us out.

It finished 1–1 but months later I was amazed to hear the claims which came from the direction of Ewood Park when the game suddenly changed its complexity. According to Blackburn it was they who had made all the running and United who had the luck.

Blackburn were fortunate that we didn't score earlier because I am sure that we would have gone on to win, and I disagree with all those Blackburn players who later in the season said we were lucky and they had outplayed us. I would say that they didn't play very well and certainly were not the best side to face us at Old Trafford.

I suppose that because we got the equalizer in the last couple of minutes you could say that we were fortunate, but it was no more than the lads deserved. If anyone has any doubts I would like them to do what I have done and sit down and study the video of the game. It is all there for anyone to see.

Immediately after the game I was asked if I felt Blackburn would prove to be a major threat to our drive for the championship, and I said that from the evidence of that Boxing Day game I didn't think they would. I also could not see us dropping enough points to let them close the gap to just goal difference, and I have to say that I was surprised it happened, but that in the end they proved themselves to be worthy challengers.

My main concern at that stage of the season was our involvement in the cup competitions. We were still in the Coca-Cola, the FA Cup was due to start for us in January, and there is always a fear that replays or postponements might add to the fixture pile-up at the end of the season.

That was still a way off as we went to Oldham for the next part of the holiday programme. The boss put me on the bench and by the time I got into the action it was all over. Seven goals had been scored, we were 5–2 up and that was the way it stayed until the end. Five goals away from home is a perfect way to come back from a so-called lucky win!

Latics are a great side to play against because, unlike the

Blackburn approach of three days earlier, they will not sit back on anything. If you score first, as we did, they come back at you.

It was Andrei Kanchelskis who got his name on the scoresheet ahead of the rest. He ignored the grassless Boundary Park pitch and showed that his speed works even on flattened mud before hitting a good shot on the run. Latics came back. They are always looking for goals and at one stage were holding us 2–2 before Steve Bruce and two from Ryan Giggs took it away from them.

It was a great pity that in the end they lost their battle to stay in the Premiership and that we played a part in their downfall. They will be missed in the top section, and I am certainly looking forward to facing them in the First Division in my new role at Middlesbrough.

So it was our home clash with Leeds and I was back in the starting line-up for the New Year's Day game. Leeds had slipped back to third place after drawing at Newcastle and at home to QPR so they knew they had to beat us to open it up again. It was another of those we-won't-score-so-neither-will-you games.

It ended 0–0, which meant we were still 12 points clear and those calculators could be put away again for the time being at least.

After Newcastle, Villa, Blackburn and Leeds – who would be the next to challenge? Liverpool. When we had studied the fixture list at the start of the season quite a few of the lads had pointed out that it looked as if the most difficult stage would come around Christmas. We all reckoned that if we could get through that period without slipping we would have done well. The end of March also looked difficult when we had to travel to Arsenal and Blackburn after away games at Wimbledon and West Ham, but there was a long way to go before then and the fixture list could change because of cup-ties.

We had stayed unbeaten in the Premiership since having that slip at Chelsea in September, and had played 17 games since then, winning 12. We knew we were producing championship form and that if we could keep up the momentum we would hold on to our trophy.

We had dropped points with that run of draws against Ipswich, Norwich, Newcastle, Blackburn and Leeds, while Rovers had started a winning streak. What hurt us most was that four of our drawn games were at home.

After Blackburn beat Chelsea to start their run-in to the holiday period, they had 5 wins out of 6 games. The only points they had dropped were against us, or should that be the other way round? I suppose to get a point at Old Trafford is an achievement, but both of us thought that we had lost two rather than gained one.

Norwich's success in Europe and the north Lancashire weather played a part in holding Rovers back slightly when their fixtures at Carrow Road and then the home game against Wimbledon had to be postponed.

We went to Anfield hoping to take advantage of this and stretch our lead, and the way we started it looked a distinct possibility. It was amazing, and a terrific advert for British football.

We were playing without Mark Hughes and Lee Sharpe who had both picked up injuries. Sparky limped off with five minutes to go against Blackburn and had been out since then, and Lee was having problems with a groin injury which was later diagnosed as a hernia and led to surgery. He played against Oldham then was out until March. I was on the bench at Anfield and looked on as the lads carried the game to Liverpool.

Liverpool should have taken the lead in the first minute but Robbie Fowler missed the target.

Nine minutes had gone when Eric Cantona floated into yards of space after drifting wide and he sent in a perfect cross which Steve Bruce ran on to. He made solid contact and headed the ball out of the reach of Bruce Grobbelaar.

Anfield was silent apart from around 1,500 United fans down in one corner of the ground. Those fans increased the volume even more 11 minutes later when Ryan Giggs took on Mark Wright. He turned the big central defender and ran at goal, chipping the ball over Bruce's head to make it 2–0.

We were attacking the Anfield Road End with the Kop in total silence behind Peter Schmeichel's goal. Three minutes later we led 3–0. We won a free kick 25 yards out and slightly left of centre. Giggsy, Incey and Eric were around the ball and it looked as if they were deciding who was going to take it.

On the bench we knew exactly what would happen. Denis Irwin took three or four strides forward and hit a beauty. The ball ripped into the top corner, bending away from Grobbelaar's fingers.

The sight of Manchester United leading 3–0 at Anfield was like waving 30,000 red rags to as many wild bulls. The Liverpool fans screamed their anger, much of it directed towards Graeme Souness.

Their players knew they would have to respond and they did so in remarkable style. Straight from the restart after that third goal they broke forward and we failed to clear the ball properly. It ran to Nigel Clough and he hit in a low, raking shot which eluded Big Peter who could have been unsighted.

There is a saying in football that when the score is 3–1 whoever gets the next goal holds the advantage. Liverpool were inspired by their break and threw everything at us. They knew that they had no option. If they could not get back into the game they would lose at home to their biggest rivals.

As far as the players are concerned we are all mates together and there are many close friends in both camps. With the supporters there is no love lost. It probably stems from the days when Liverpool dominated the First Division yet found it impossible to get one over on United on any regular basis. They were undeniably the top team in the country, yet during that period we held an Indian sign over them and in the 20 league games we played against one another in the 1980s Liverpool only won twice.

It was a similar story in the FA Cup where we met in the semi-finals a couple of times, so it was understandable that the frustration crept in. Add to that the popularity of United, who attracted the biggest crowds despite Liverpool's success, and you had the perfect recipe for rivalry.

Who would score next? We went close, then another mistake in our defence gave Nigel Clough a shot on goal. He struck it well from the edge of the box and suddenly Liverpool were back in the game.

Half-time was approaching and after leading 3–0 we were up against it! What do you say to your players in that situation?

The boss could really add little to what the lads already knew. We were playing well enough and the pace was hectic. All we could do was to try to tighten our defence and make sure that we didn't concede another goal. If we could hold them back for a while we might be able to re-establish our attacks and get a fourth. If we did, that surely would be the end for them.

The gaffer described Liverpool's attitude during that second period as 'kamikaze', and he was right. It was total suicide football as the Kop screamed frantically. Graeme Souness who a few weeks later was to lose his job as Liverpool's manager, was known to have a heart condition, and after watching those last 45 minutes I could understand why.

There were crunching tackles from both sides, with Paul Ince coming through as my man of the match, and the more the minutes ticked away the more we thought we had done it. Liverpool were under pressure and all we had to do was keep things as they were and we were home and dry.

I did a few warm-up runs on the track alongside the pitch accompanied by Darren Ferguson and Les Sealey, our other subs. The Liverpool fans made us feel welcome by yelling abuse in our direction. The boss said later that he didn't use any substitutes because he thought it would have been difficult for the new player to adjust to the pace. Unless there was an injury the warming-up was unnecessary.

Liverpool made one switch and it turned out to be crucial. Nigel Clough had scored two, been booked and run himself ragged. He was taken off and replaced by Stig Bjornebye. With the 10 minutes remaining the Norwegian helped to create an opening on our right, floated over a cross and Neil Ruddock got his head to it and scored.

Unbelievable. From 3–0 up to 3–3, and in the last 10 minutes both sides battled away to grab the winning goal. Perhaps it was justice that it never came.

The gaffer said afterwards it had been the first time in his managerial career one of his teams had thrown away a 3–0 lead but he was stunned rather than angry. It was one of those once-in-a-lifetime games which didn't need a winner.

We had now played 25 Premiership games and had 58 points. Blackburn had 2 games in hand and were 13 points behind us. On the form they were showing they would win those spare games, so realistically our lead was 7 points. We knew we had to tread warily.

Then came a break from the demands of the Premiership as the top clubs played their first games in the FA Cup. We had known for a month we were due to go back to Bramall Lane for another tie against Sheffield United.

It was a repeat of the previous season's 5th Round and we were determined that the result would not be the same. Then we had been knocked out as Steve Bruce missed an 84th-minute penalty. It was a sickener, but at least it freed us from fixture congestion and gave us a clear road to the championship.

Our tie at Sheffield was another Sunday afternoon game staged for the demands of television. The previous day Blackburn had drawn with Portsmouth and the replay meant an extra game for them. That made us all the more determined to win through at the first attempt.

Once again I watched from the bench as the lads battled away in a scrappy affair. We didn't seem to be able to put our passing together in the usual way. Sparky had come back after his injury and once again we had Andrei wide on the right and Ryan on the left.

Sheffield battled hard and there were a few clashes on and off the ball. It was one of these which led to the game's most controversial moment. Before then, with just over an hour gone, we had one of our best moves.

Mark Hughes began it with a pass out to Paul Parker, who found Paul Ince, and there was a neat exchange between him and Eric Cantona before the ball came back to Sparky who hit in a powerful shot from a narrow angle. We were in front, and that turned out to be the only goal.

Thirteen minutes later the frustration of taking a few nudges and kicks, most of them unseen by the referee, led to Mark getting his marching orders. He and David Tuttle chased the ball as it ran towards the Sheffield corner flag. Sparky suddenly and quite openly kicked Tuttle up the backside.

All hell broke loose and Gerald Ashby, who had already booked Mark, produced both cards out of his pockets. A second yellow, then red, and Mark had a long walk to the dressing-room from the farthest corner of the ground.

Why did he do it? 'I don't know, I suppose you could call it a rush of blood,' was Sparky's assessment. It was a burst of impetuosity he found hard to explain. He had been pushed to the brink and could take no more.

The television boys had a field day. Mark was put under the microscope and so began our branding as a dirty side. It was trial by television. The cameras were constantly at our games, and not only did the anti-United brigade react because they thought we were getting too much coverage, incidents which are commonplace in most games were enlarged out of all proportion by the armchair critics.

Close-ups of players reacting to referees' decisions were used to accuse us of whingeing. But why? Find me a professional player who has never questioned a decision if you can. Of course players dispute rulings, of course they use what is sometimes described as industrial language during a game, but Manchester United do it no more or less than any other club.

If you point fingers at United, then also point at the rest because every club is the same, and so is virtually every player. It is too late to change things. Unless a rule was introduced which said that it was an offence to speak out of turn during a game, football will stay as it is. There is a lot at stake and a wrong decision can have a big influence on the outcome of a game and that is why passions run so high.

What amazes me is that the controversies on television are more often than not sparked off by former professionals. The way they preach you would think that they had been absolute angels when they played. Certainly that is the case if they can stand up and say that they never did similar things themselves.

Did Jimmy Hill never foul an opponent? Did Ian St John never dispute a referee's decision? Did Alan Hansen never retaliate? Did Jimmy Greaves never swear during a game? Shown in close-up on television, any moment of anxiety, any incident which sparks a reaction, can seem like a serious offence.

Sparky did wrong and was punished. He committed a foul and was sent off and later suspended. We did not need to see the incident time and again, but that and others which were to come later in the season were held up as the 'other side' of Manchester United.

Mark's goal won us the game and another tough tie lay ahead. We were drawn away to Norwich.

We were now settling into a regular pattern of weekend-midweek-weekend games because of cup commitments, and I was back in the side three days after the trip to Sheffield. Portsmouth came to Old Trafford for the 5th Round of the Coca-Cola Cup, and with Paul Ince ill, Brian McClair joined me in midfield. Roy Keane was on the bench along with Dion Dublin and Les Sealey.

Pompey had been going well in Division One and were being tipped for promotion. They played some lively football, with Paul Walsh looking a threat. He has always been one of those players who enjoys the big occasion and in front of a crowd of close on 44,000 he was back in his Liverpool or Tottenham days, running at our defence and showing that he still had plenty to offer.

Ryan Giggs scored the first of the night, created by Mark Hughes winning the ball in midfield. But Walshy was on target 4 minutes later when he got the Pompey equalizer. It came from a corner taken by Alan McLoughlin, one of our former apprentices who had moved on. It was a near-post header, not the kind of goal you want to give away, and it took us another half-hour before we were back in the lead.

This time Eric Cantona got his head to a cross from Paul Parker. Pompey, and Paul Walsh, were far from finished. They fought hard and in the 70th minute Peter Schmeichel made a save from a Darryl Powell cross. He couldn't hold the ball and Walsh was there to score with another header.

The boss was far from pleased, pointing out that the smallest forward on the field had beaten our defenders in the air not once, but twice. Now we, like Blackburn, had an unwanted replay to contend with.

Before that game came two important Premiership games. After having that run of 4 draws in 6 games we knew we had to get back to winning.

Firstly we were away to Tottenham, a club which was going through all sorts of traumas after being involved in a High Court case which followed the dismissal of Chief Executive Terry Venables. He and Alan Sugar had battled for control at White Hart Lane with Terry losing out, and the fans were still in a restless mood. Many of them backed the former player against the businessman and it created an uneasy atmosphere at the Tottenham ground.

Terry was on his way back after the courtroom upset and was on the verge of being handed the England manager's job – he prefers to be known as the coach – as we went to London and won 1–0 thanks to another goal from Mark Hughes. It was our 10th away win out of 13.

While we were winning at Tottenham, Blackburn beat Sheffield United 2–1 at Bramall Lane with Alan Shearer getting both their goals, and the top of the table was:

	P	W	D	L	F	A	pts
Manchester United	26	18	7	1	53	23	61
Blackburn Rovers	24	14	6	4	34	19	48

As we drove back from Tottenham I little realized what a week of mixed emotions lay ahead. It began when the speculation surrounding Terry Venables and England strengthened, with my name being linked to a post as his assistant. It ended with football in mourning following the death of Sir Matt Busby.

When we had played Sheffield United in the FA Cup the news had reached us that Sir Matt was in hospital. He had a blood clot removed from his leg and appeared to be recovering. Then his condition suddenly deteriorated. On Thursday 20 January he died peacefully in his hospital bed, surrounded by his family.

Manchester wept.

That night tributes poured in as the news was broadcast and next morning when we arrived at The Cliff for training there was a strange silence about the whole place.

We were devastated. Every player knew Sir Matt even though none of us had actually played under him.

He was a father-figure at Old Trafford and we all knew that everything Manchester United had become was linked to his days as manager. He had been responsible for laying the foundations of today's success, and had also built the club's reputation for entertaining football which hopefully we were continuing.

Sir Matt was a wonderful warm man. I will never forget the times I have been in his company, from the day I first arrived as a player to the moment we stood together celebrating the championship which ended his 26-year wait. That moment we shared when he came into the dressing-room to offer us his congratulations is one I will always cherish.

Another of my fondest memories was when we went on a European trip and he talked to us about how great British football was and how British players were the best. By the time he had finished he had us all convinced. We went out onto the pitch knowing Manchester United really was the best, and it made me realize what an effect he must have had on his players during the time he was in charge. No wonder they achieved so much.

He had a way with people, and he had the time for everyone. Now he had gone.

At The Cliff fans gathered in silent groups, while at Old Trafford a sea of flowers, scarves and other souvenirs brought by a stream of supporters were laid under the Munich clock, a reminder of another sad time in the club's history. Older supporters wept openly, there were tears in the eyes of the so-called hard-nosed media men, and the boss had a tough job on his hands lifting a muted dressing-room.

He handled things superbly. He got us out on the field and down to some hard work. He knew there would be extra demands from the media, and made himself available for endless televison and radio interviews. He answered a flood of telephone calls and comforted supporters who were obviously distressed.

He also made a most amazing statement regarding the game against Everton which was coming up the following day:

'It's going to be a hard time for everyone at the club and you only have to look at the way people have been gathering here this morning, and at Old Trafford, to see what Sir Matt means to Manchester United.

'Great is a word that is often over used in football, but not as far as Sir Matt was concerned.

'He was a great manager.

'He was great for Manchester United and he was a great man.

'As far as my team talk tomorrow is concerned, all I will say to the players is, "Go out and play the way he would have wanted you to". As for the result, that doesn't matter, I want to see a game of football that Sir Matt would be proud of.'

Alex said it all. We were in contention for the championship, we were at home, but the Everton game would be about football not simply winning.

I said that it was a week of mixed emotions, because coinciding with the tragic news came an approach from the Football Association asking if I wanted to be involved in the new England set-up. Jimmy Armfield had been appointed as a liaison man by the FA and he had made the initial approach. How would I react if the FA invited me to join the England backroom staff?

The news leaked and that morning at The Cliff I found myself being targeted for two lines of questioning. It was difficult to adjust. One moment I was being asked to pay tribute to Sir Matt, and the next to comment about my future. Would I accept the post of England's number two if it was offered to me?

I knew that it would not be very long before I would have to make an important decision about my future but that morning was not the time. My reply was that I would give an answer if and when the official offer came.

At that time there was no England manager, and under the circumstances it seemed inappropriate for me to talk about how I might or might not react. There were other things on my mind and uppermost was the loss of someone of great importance to my club.

I would dearly have loved to have played in the Everton game but instead found myself looking on as a spectacle of football and emotion unfolded. Old Trafford was subdued during the build-up to the game and when the teams came out they were led by a lone piper. You could have heard a pin drop as the music echoed from the overhanging roof of the packed stadium.

The players reached the centre circle and the referee's whistle signalled the start of a minute's silence. I am sure that I speak on behalf of every United supporter who was in the ground that day when I say that the Everton fans were a credit to their club. There was not a word spoken during the two or three minutes building up to the silence itself, and in that 60 seconds not even the birds sang.

It was as if the whole of Manchester was paying its silent respects to Sir Matt.

Football rivalry can at times be intense and for players it is often difficult to understand. I have countless friends in the game who play for other clubs. We are rivals on the field, during a game we want to come out on top, but afterwards we remain friends.

Supporters seem to find this impossible, but that afternoon I am sure that Manchester United and Everton followers came a little closer to one another.

As for the game, it was everything Sir Matt would have wanted, and while there was only one goal it was certainly a fitting tribute to a man who loved football with flair.

We had endless chances, with Eric Cantona, Andrei Kanchelskis and Ryan Giggs turning on a display of remarkable skill, speed and control, with Giggsy scoring in the 26th minute. Neville Southall was outstanding in the Everton goal and as the crowd chanted 'Busby, Busby!', the great man was remembered in style.

A day later Blackburn and Leeds met at Elland Road, with Leeds fans disgracing themselves by disrupting the silence for Sir Matt. It was a total embarrassment for Leeds United and Gordon Strachan admitted afterwards: 'We were so stunned by what happened it probably cost us the game. We felt such shame we could not play and I suppose the truth was we didn't want to after that.'

Gordon and Leeds skipper Gary McAllister were amongst the mourners who attended Sir Matt's funeral four days after Blackburn's 2–1 victory. The whole of our squad was amongst the players past and present who filled Our Lady and St John's Church in Chorlton-cum-Hardy for the Requiem Mass.

We had flown back from Portsmouth after playing in the replay of our Coca-Cola Cup tie at Fratton Park the previous night. It was a game we could have done without but we had won thanks to a goal from Brian McClair. I think it is fair to say that after their display at Old Trafford we expected more from Portsmouth, but that single goal was enough, and so on a rain-soaked morning we found ourselves in Sir Matt's parish church as outside the streets were lined for miles with thousands of mourners.

George Best, Bobby Charlton, Denis Law and others from the European Cup-winning side of 1968 were there, together with players from Sir Matt's 1948 and 1963 FA Cup-winning teams, and his championship winners of 1952, 1956, 1957, 1965 and 1967. All were there to pay their respects.

It was a time for everyone to think of the past, but we could also look to the future, and the players of the present decided there could be no better tribute to Sir Matt than to retain our championship, and if possible improve on it by completing the elusive double.

That was now our target.

CHAPTER FIVE

Treble Chance

IT WAS THE LAST SUNDAY OF JANUARY WHEN THE LADS RAN OUT to face Norwich in the FA Cup at Carrow Road. A bitterly cold wind blew in from the North Sea making things unpleasant for the fans, and its gusts meant that at times control was difficult for the players.

As soon as the game got under way everyone seemed to forget the wintry conditions and the supporters spent most of their time off their seats as play flowed from one end to the other. It was a good old-fashioned cup-tie, a battle from start to finish.

I was forced to watch things from the wings once again after having more hospital treatment for my sinus problem. We had Mark Hughes back to lead the attack after he had missed the Portsmouth replay because of his one-match ban, and although we didn't know it at the time, we were going to have to get used to suspensions causing us selection problems in the weeks ahead.

Mark's ban had come after his sending off against Sheffield United, and he was destined to miss the Norwich tie until we drew against Pompey. That brought the ban forward and he was ready for action against The Canaries.

Brian McClair and Dion Dublin were on the bench with Les Sealey and we started the game with this line-up:

Schmeichel
Parker Bruce Pallister Irwin
Kanchelskis Keane Ince Giggs
Hughes Cantona

We were again under television scrutiny as the tie had been switched to please the millions who enjoy their football after Sunday lunch. They saw a Manchester United determined to get through to Round Five as well as being left with something to chew on for the rest of the week.

Norwich were under new management. John Deehan had taken over from Mike Walker, who was now installed at Everton and had already tasted disappointment. The Toffees were one of the big boys who had fallen by the FA Cup's wayside. They went out to Bolton Wanderers, who had a great cup run disposing of Arsenal and Aston Villa before reaching the quarter-finals, where they were pipped by Oldham.

At one time in his playing career John Deehan had a spell with Manchester City and they too were in the news that weekend. Francis Lee had taken over as their new chairman following months of haranguing. He replaced Peter Swales after a hate campaign by the Maine Road fans. It was an incredible period in the city. The headlines in the *Manchester Evening News* were either screaming out about our success, or telling everybody about the problems at Maine Road. I don't think there could ever have been as great a gap between the two rivals.

There was a lot of take-over talk, with the Francis Lee consortium said to be ready to plunge £10 million into the club, while

United's shares broke through the £6 barrier and were pushing towards £7. We had been valued at more than £100 million *plus* the players – ten times bigger than City.

The Blues fans could not take it. Their protests drove Peter Swales away and I am sure they all thought that when Franny stepped in he would simply wave a magic wand and all would be well again.

Football is never as simple as that and Franny's star-dust didn't have time to settle. The Blues had been knocked out of the cup the day before our tie, when they were away to Cardiff. It was one of the few Fourth Round games which had reached a conclusion .

Blackburn had to replay against Charlton after a goalless draw at The Valley, and Leeds were also involved in a second game after managing to survive against Oxford. They had a tough fight and had to come back from behind twice at the Manor Ground.

Ipswich were through, knocking out Tottenham. So were Aston Villa and Wimbledon. Now we wanted to be the fourth Premiership side to make sure of a place in Round Five.

Norwich obviously had the same idea and reverted to their normal style of attacking play. They had home advantage and wanted to show their supporters that those two Carrow Road defeats were history. They fancied their chances, and there was an extra edge to their game as they were out to show their new manager that they could fight.

It was attack, attack, attack, and there were one or two dodgy tackles flying around too. Only a couple of minutes had gone when one of the Norwich players had a dig at Eric Cantona. It was one of those 'just-to-let-you-know-I'm-here' challenges, and there was a quick reaction not from Eric but from Roy Keane. It earned him a yellow card.

That meant that with only five minutes gone we had a player walking the tightrope and it was more evidence against us in the case being prepared by the television archives.

We held off the early pressure, then Keano got his name in the notebook again – this time under the heading 'scorer.' Ryan Giggs began the move with a great solo run, before laying off a pass for Andrei Kanchelskis. He found Roy with a good pass, and with 19 minutes gone he put us in front. He took the goal well, keeping his head and sending in a low powerful shot which Bryan Gunn could not stop.

The flair of Eric Cantona produced the second and we knew we were were comfortably through. However, it was not our tremendous away victory which made the news. No, it was an incident involving Eric Cantona and John Polston.

Leading up to it Eric had been very lucky to survive two attempts to elbow him. Both had gone unnoticed by the officials. Polston was not the offender although he too had been niggling the Frenchman.

Eric was aware of everything that was going on even if the referee seemed reluctant to take any action.

Then came a chase to the goal-line at the Norwich end. Eric was first in but the pace of the ball beat him and it ran out of play. He and the defender crossed the line together and Eric was aware that he had an opponent coming in from behind. He prepared himself either to get a kick on the back of the leg or to be pushed into the advertising boards but decided to strike first and ask questions later.

However, as Eric put the brakes on in front of Polston, the Norwich man fell. Eric flicked out a crafty back-heel. In all honesty I think he was trying to whack him on the shins or at least protect himself from being caught down the back of the calf by Polston. But because the defender had fallen Eric's kick caught him between the shoulder blades.

It was not a 'mule kick', as it was later described by some sources. If he had used the same power to back-heel a ball it would not have reached the edge of the penalty area. But at the same time he was wrong.

It was not life-threatening or anywhere close to being as serious as that, but the local fans went bananas. They yelled for Eric's head, but like the elbows earlier it went unnoticed by the officials.

Not by the television cameras though. Eric was given the slow-motion action replay treatment. 'Let's see that again from a different angle.'

In the press box few had seen anything although all were aware from the crowd's reaction that something was amiss. Descriptions came back from the newspaper offices where they were watching TV and they were off! Eric took a slamming but he was not alone.

When the game ended Jimmy Hill and his BBC cronies laid into Eric demanding everything but the guillotine. Jimmy was in his element, preaching to the masses about the rights and wrongs of Cantona's game. He referred to him as 'nothing more than a brat'.

The story then switches to the after-match press conference where the remark was relayed to Alex as he faced the media. His reply, which I am sure he meant to be one of those off-the-record replies every manager makes from time to time, was picked up and used by the tabloids. 'Jimmy Hill is a pratt!'

Zoom! The rocket was launched and there followed a week of comment and counter-comment in the national press and on television. Eric was given the full treatment and I am positive it led to some of the problems he faced later in the season. He was a marked man, and every time he touched the ball faced the wrath of the opposition supporters.

Once again it posed the question: who is running the game, the football authorities or television?

Eric was wrong. He committed a foul and got away with it. I am not arguing about that. As a professional footballer I can fully understand what led to it. You can only take so much and there are times when you react to situations, then regret your reaction later. If players kick you and elbow you it takes a tolerant person not to react in some way. Eric thought he had the chance to get a bit of his own back.

The referee and linesmen missed the incident or chose to ignore it because they know things like that happen so often during a game. Anyone with any doubts need only take a good look the next time they attend a game. When there is a corner or a free kick which will send the ball into the penalty area, watch what goes on 'off' the ball.

They will see many personal battles for supremacy as players try to get one over their opponent. There are little digs and ankle taps, verbal threats, nudges and pushes. This goes on in every professional game and at just about every other level too.

How do you stop it? Take physical contact out of football?

As it turned out Eric was booked for a later challenge when he jumped two-footed into an opponent, but of course the television evidence showed he had been lucky. Two bookable offences would have led to a sending off.

According to the Norwich supporters it was the second time he had escaped punishment in a game against their side. Television backed their claims as it linked this incident to a moment during the league game at Old Trafford when Eric pulled down an opponent. 'Is there one rule for Eric Cantona and Manchester United and another for the rest of football? Are referees scared to punish United?' came the cry.

You have got to be joking. Television has an important role to play in bringing football to a wide audience, but it must not be allowed to take control. As long as football decides that the referee is the sole judge of what happens during a game, using the support of his linesmen, then there is no need for any outside agencies to influence things.

We all know that referees make mistakes, and that their errors have created problems on the pitch and off it, but highlighting them is not the solution. If the referee takes no action, he has decided that there is no action to be taken.

If football is to be controlled by television then let there be cameras at every game and let players be suspended and goals rubbed out or results changed by action replays. Would anybody truly want that to happen?

Every player, and I imagine every supporter, knows that in the course of a season, and perhaps even in as short a time span as the 90 minutes of a game, decisions can go both for and against your side. You may not agree with an offside, you may think the referee is harsh to award a free kick or a penalty, but there is nothing you can do to change his judgement.

We have had goals scored against us which would not have been allowed had television evidence been used, and I am sure that some of our opponents would make the same claim against us. It is all part of football.

So is the off-the-ball stuff. Players don't condone it, but we accept it.

Manchester United have been subjected to a goldfish-bowl existence for the past few years, and since the advent of satellite television – which incidentally doesn't quite have the same self-opinionated approach as the BBC – the number of times our games are screened has increased. We haven't asked for such attention although you would think from the number of complaints I have heard that we demanded to be on the box every week.

Once upon a time football would be on television once or twice a week. Now it is available every day and every player knows he is being watched, but Big Brother has to have some leniency in his approach. Show the game by all means, warts and all, but don't just concentrate on the warts!

Television had another role to play that afternoon because no sooner had our Carrow Road tie finished than the draw for Round Five was screened.

We knew it. It had to happen. After all the hoo-ha that afternoon we were drawn away from home again – against Wimbledon at Selhurst Park. Another away tie, another televised game and a five o'clock kick-off on a Sunday. They really do consider the travelling supporters, don't they?

We knew that keeping our pledge to the memory of Sir Matt would be difficult, and it was turning out that way, but I don't suppose he would have wanted it any other way.

Our away form in the Premiership continued as we went to Loftus Road on the Saturday following our trip to Norwich and faced a lively Queen's Park Rangers. Andrei Kanchelskis was on top form. He scored the first goal after 18 minutes in a move started by Peter Schmeichel. He launched one of his huge throws downfield, Paul Ince flicked it on, and Andrei chased in at full speed and fired it home.

Then – and there is a hint of irony about this – QPR equalized from the penalty spot after a foul that never was. Roy Keane and Gary Penrice were chasing the ball in our box when the Rangers' player tripped and fell. Roy never touched him and you could tell by Gary's expression that he was annoyed with himself. He felt he had lost the chance of creating a goal, but that despair turned to delight when referee Graham Poll pointed to the spot.

Ironic? Yes, you've guessed it, television proved that it was anything but a penalty. From the referee's angle it probably looked as though Roy had pushed Gary in the back but the camera showed quite clearly that nothing like that had happened. Penrice simply lost his balance and there was no physical contact, but it was an illustration of the way decisions go both for and against you.

Needless to say Clive Wilson scored and QPR could not believe their luck, they had been given a goal by a refereeing error, but they knew that before the season was finished they would no doubt be refused one.

We had to start again and amazingly right from the kick-off we ran through their defence and scored our second. Eric headed in his 17th of the season thanks to some quick thinking from Denis Irwin. He had taken a free kick just outside the Rangers' box and fired in a shot which rebounded off their wall. He picked up the ball, ran to the goal-line and chipped over a lovely cross which had the QPR defence in a panic. Eric came in on the far post and nodded the ball home.

Ryan Giggs made it 3–1 in the 59th minute with a lovely solo effort in which he beat three men before taking the ball wide to the left and shooting from the angle. Then Les Ferdinand put us under pressure for the last 20 minutes when he pulled another back, but we were comfortably home despite that bit of first-half luck which had gone Rangers way.

We led the table by 10 points but we had played one game more than Blackburn, who beat Wimbledon 3–0 that afternoon.

From the FA Cup to the Premiership, and now we had to prepare for the Coca-Cola Cup. With Wembley a game away the boss named an unchanged side as Sheffield Wednesday came to Old Trafford for yet another Sunday game.

Trevor Francis and I have been close friends for many years and I knew he would have something up his sleeve for the first leg of the semi-final. I was still out and anxious to get back in the side but after three successive away wins I knew it would be hard. So I was again a spectator as Wednesday threw a blanket over midfield.

They tried to hold us out and hit us on the break knowing that they had home advantage to come in the second-leg. It almost worked. We got our chance to spoil their plans when Roland Nilsson tried to pass back to his goalkeeper. The full-back slipped as he hit the ball and Ryan Giggs pounced.

He was flying. He ran into the Wednesday box and showed his growing confidence by rounding Kevin Pressman. It looked as though he had taken the ball too far, but from the narrowest of angles he rolled it into the net. It was a smashing goal and similar to our third against QPR. This time it turned out to be the only one of the afternoon.

I was having treatment and working my way back to full fitness, along with Lee Sharpe who was building up following his operation. The rest of the squad was preparing for the FA Cup-tie against The Dons when the news came through that Terry Venables had decided on his new backroom staff – and I was included.

Terry wanted me as his number two on the England coaching staff. I was offered the post on a part-time basis, meaning I could carry on playing for United at least until the end of the season, and I was delighted to accept.

I could hardly wait. Eventually Terry called his first squad together and I was invited down to Bisham Abbey to work with the lads. I enjoyed every minute and it made me realize where my future lay. It was my first step towards management.

Decision time was getting closer by the day. I cannot remember ever having dreams of being a football manager, certainly not as a young boy. My only ambition then was to become a professional footballer.

The target has changed constantly throughout my career – getting into the reserves, then the first team at West Brom, playing for England at different levels, moving to United, then becoming captain of club and country. These were all personal milestones which gave me something to aim at in the various stages of my playing career.

As I got older the targets had changed. Now I knew the direction I wanted my future to go. I had made it to the top as a player, my ambition was to do the same as a manager.

Terry Venables took over the England job when morale was at a fairly low ebb. Our aim was to get back to where we had been before the slump and then go on from there.

English international football had taken a hammering during the days when Graham Taylor was in charge. Our failure to qualify for the 1994 World Cup finals brought matters to a head. Something had to be done and the FA took the necessary action, but I honestly felt that we could turn things round quickly, that the players were there but had not been used.

I believe there are many good young players coming through in the Premiership, English players who will make it at international level, and I am convinced that we have enough skill and talent to do well in the 1996 European Championships. By then I hope we will have created a strong backbone to our international set-up, which has got to be our main aim. That and our efforts to see the game being played the way we feel it should be played.

I was glad when Middlesbrough later agreed to my being able to continue with my England post, because I feel that each role can be of benefit to the other. I hope the day isn't far away when England players will play for Middlesbrough, and perhaps more to the point, when Middlesbrough players will play for England!

During the period before the England changes were announced there had been some happenings in the FA Cup which were not necessarily going to work in our favour. Blackburn were knocked out by Charlton Athletic in a replay at Ewood Park. Apparently the First Division club had been unlucky not to finish the job off the first time and the 1–0 win put them through for an away tie at Bristol City. Arsenal were also out, along with Leeds and Newcastle.

Our rivals for the championship could now have a clear run at things while we were still being tipped for the treble. Would the pattern of the previous two seasons be followed?

The build-up to the Wimbledon game was exactly what we expected. The Dons' claims made a lot of back page reading during the week. They were ready for anything we could produce and were confident they could end our unbeaten run, which now stretched back an amazing 31 games to that night when we slipped at Stoke.

Joe Kinnear, the Wimbledon boss, took his players back to Plough Lane for a training session, 'to remind them of their roots!', and we knew they would be fired up. Brian McClair and Dion Dublin were again on the bench as the lads tore Wimbledon to shreds. They played some scintillating football which had the Sky experts drooling and Eric Cantona was at his best.

He scored the first and it was sheer class. Wimbledon were under pressure as we attacked down the left. Denis Irwin floated over a good cross aimed for a runner coming in at the far post. Gary Elkins, the left full-back, got there first and headed it clear of the penalty area straight into the path of Eric. He flicked the ball up, then hit in a dipping drive all in the same movement and it brought a gasp from the crowd before the cheers broke out.

Paul Ince got the second with a near-post header from a Giggs corner, beating Gary Pallister to the ball into the bargain, but the goal of the game came from Denis Irwin. No fewer than fifteen passes created the opening for him to run in from the left edge of the box, beat a defender like a world-class winger, and slot the ball home.

He showed what a great little player he is. Denis is one of those quiet lads around the dressing-room, perhaps he is naturally shy but on the field he has turned into one of the best full-backs in the game. He is a natural right-sided player, but has been switched to the left to become outstanding at full-back. His contribution as a goal scorer has increased along with his confidence and the goal at Selhurst Park was the third of four he got during the season, much to the annoyance of Paul Parker who was our only regular outfielder not to score!

It took us comfortably through to the Sixth Round, and we listened intently as the names came out in the draw. 'Manchester United . . .' we knew we had a home draw at last '. . . will play Bristol City or Charlton.' Not bad. We were all quite happy with the prospect.

Earlier that afternoon Bolton pulled off another shock by disposing of Aston Villa at Burnden Park and became the team nobody fancied playing. Against all odds they had won replays at Goodison and Highbury and got the town of Bolton buzzing. The fans there wanted a repeat of the 1958 final, and we were quite happy to let them have their dreams.

We had just passed Chinese New Year, The Year of the Dog, and the sports-page headline writers turned 1994 into 'The Year of the Underdog'. The Premiership clubs were dropping like flies to the First Division sides, but we had no intentions of being bitten by Charlton. Oldham had also got through, as had Chelsea and West Ham who were joined by Wolves and Luton.

Things were getting tighter in the Premiership. Thanks to a run of 7 consecutive wins, followed by a draw at Norwich,

Blackburn had closed the gap to 6 points. By 26 February they had played a game more than us.

That day we were away to West Ham, and Blackburn were across London at Arsenal. We drew 2–2 but what went on during that game at Upton Park sickened me and left me fuming.

It was Paul Ince's return. He was playing against his old club for the first time since his move to Old Trafford. He had been disappointed to miss the game against them in 1992 and had been looking forward to this one from the day the Hammers had won promotion. It turned out to be a day he would rather forget, but not because of the result.

Throughout the afternoon he was subjected to racial taunts from the very fans who once worshipped him. He was jeered every time he touched the ball and there was no-one more delighted than me when he got our equalizer 3 minutes from time. I just wish it had been the winner. No player should have to endure what Paul had to go through that day and I only hope that the mindless morons who were responsible will grow to regret their actions. Supporters like that don't deserve a great club like West Ham.

There was a bright side to the afternoon, and it gave us all a good laugh when we heard about it as we sat on the coach ready for the trip back to Manchester. We had gone to London without Ryan Giggs, who pulled out of the squad the day before with a slight hamstring problem. He stayed behind for extra treatment but the boss had told no-one outside the club.

Alex didn't want West Ham to find out, because he knew they could adjust their game plan. We had all been sworn to secrecy, but there was a leak. Two hours before the game a listener to Piccadilly Radio's *Saturday Sport* programme broke the news on the air ahead of Tom Tyrrell, the match commentator.

Tom had been tipped off by the gaffer through David Meek of the *Manchester Evening News* and was 'sitting' on the story until the teams were announced. However Ryan was spotted at The Cliff earlier in the day by the supporter, who had gone to the 'A' team game. The station broadcast the story during their phone-in and most of Manchester already knew he would be missing.

It reminded me of the night Mark Hughes was acting as

Tom's comments man for our European Cup-Winners' Cup-tie at Wrexham. Sparky was injured and during the commentary was asked about his progress: 'I'm coming along fine and I'll be fit for Saturday, but we're keeping it quiet!' he told his audience.

We all knew Ryan was in Manchester, but even so a rumour spread like bushfire when the team sheets went up. 'Giggs has done a runner, he's gone missing.'

Many comparisons have been made between Giggsy and George Best but this was taking things too far. Apparently half of the Upton Park press box were convinced that Ryan had walked out on the club, and even those who knew the truth began to wonder if something was wrong.

Fed with this information the boss had a field day at the after-match conference.

'What about Ryan Giggs?' was the question.

'Don't know where he is,' replied the boss, 'he's gone missing . . .'

There was a pause. Total silence followed, and a shuffling of feet as 'what-did-I-tell-you' nudges were exchanged. Alex couldn't keep his face straight, and burst out laughing. He enjoyed his moment. There is nothing he likes better than winding up the press.

We had only drawn, but Blackburn lost at Highbury and our lead increased to 7 points:

	P	W	D	L	F	A	PTS
Manchester United	29	20	8	1	59	27	68
Blackburn Rovers	30	18	7	5	44	23	61
Arsenal	30	13	12	5	34	16	51

Ryan was fit again for our next game but there was a price to pay for the point at West Ham. Eric Cantona picked up a calf strain and was ruled out as we came to the second leg of the Coca-Cola Cup semi-final.

I was back on the bench but it was another case of looking on while those around me turned on a special display. It was possibly one of our best performances of the season and we tore Sheffield Wednesday apart.

The game should have been staged on 23 February but heavy

snow in the Pennines had made driving conditions hazardous, and even though the Hillsborough pitch was playable, the game was postponed. For once common sense prevailed.

A week later the thaw set in and we reached melting point. Our critics felt that one-goal lead from the first leg might not be enough and we expected a tough game from Wednesday.

Their season hung on them doing well. They were 24 points behind us in the Premiership, had gone out of the FA Cup to Chelsea in Round Four, and were no doubt hoping that things would go better with Coca-Cola!

Wishful thinking. Within 4 minutes we were ahead through Brian McClair, after 10 it was 2–0, and even though Hyde pulled a goal back, the demolition was completed by Mark Hughes. He gave us a 3–1 half-time lead, then topped things off by cracking in a fourth in the second half.

We won 4–1 on the night, 5–1 on aggregate. It was our 18th away win of the season, and by reaching the Wembley final we were bang on course for part one of the treble.

Standing in our way would be Ron Atkinson's Aston Villa, whose semi-final against an unlucky Tranmere Rovers was packed with controversy. Villa 'keeper Mark Bosnich was lucky to stay on the field after bringing down John Aldridge as he closed in on goal. Then Mark finished up their hero as he saved a crucial spot kick during the penalty shoot-out which decided who would go to Wembley.

'Funny old game,' someone once said, and those words were never more true.

Villa had been lucky not to have their goalkeeper sent off but by the time we met them at Wembley our first-choice 'keeper was suspended because he did receive his marching orders in an earlier game.

Peter Schmeichel got his red card in the Sixth Round of the FA Cup and it came a week after a major upset. Our unbeaten run had been stretched to 34 games when Chelsea came to Old Trafford.

Chelsea, the only side to beat us in the Premiership, turned out to be the bogey men of 1994 and did it again, this time in front of our own supporters. It was unbelievable really. We dominated the game from start to finish but Chelsea went home with 3 points.

I only played the last 9 minutes, after seeing Chelsea steal their win when Gavin Peacock scored, just as he had done at Stamford Bridge. The goal came in the 64th minute after we had made all of the play. We had no alternative but to throw everything into attack but somehow Chelsea held out.

We found it hard to believe and with Blackburn winning 2–0 at home to Liverpool our lead was cut to just 4 points. They had played a game more than us but we were almost within reach.

Big Peter's sending off the following Saturday was one he might have got away with had there not been so much publicity about other similar incidents. We had seen 'keepers handling the ball outside the box, or pulling down opponents with the so-called 'professional foul', and getting away with it. Not this time.

Referee Robbie Hart found Peter guilty on two counts. He decided that not only did he deliberately handle the ball when he came out of his area to stop Charlton's Kim Grant, but he fouled him as well. It was not the first time we would see the red card in the weeks which followed.

There was a bit of anger amongst the lads as we left the field at half-time. We thought the Charlton player had made a lot of the challenge and influenced the referee, but nobody argued after we saw the action replay.

We were down to ten men and faced the possibility of going out of the Cup, Blackburn were breathing down our necks in the League – the odds were beginning to stack up against us, yet you could sense the determination. There was no way we would let things slip after setting the pace for such a long time, and if Charlton thought it might be easy in the second half they were in for a shock.

Peter had been sent off in the 45th minute. A few seconds more and the referee would have blown for the break. In the confusion which followed the boss juggled things round. He sent on Les Sealey to take over in goal, but as a substitute for Paul Parker. Quite the normal thing to do, but a move which angered the United knockers.

Why? They thought it unfair that a sent-off 'keeper should be replaced by another goalie. I can see nothing wrong with that and it has nothing to do with it working in our favour on this occasion.

If a team has a striker sent off and have their second string centre-forward on the bench, would anyone object to a manager putting on his replacement front man and taking off a defender or midfielder? Why have a reserve goalkeeper on the bench if he cannot be used in this way? The boss sacrificed a defender so that he could have a skilled 'keeper in goal, unlike the days before substitutes when one of the outfield players would have taken over.

I suppose that is what the anti-United brigade wanted, to see us playing with someone like Roy Keane in the nets, using his Gaelic football skills. Even then I reckon we would still have won.

Charlton threatened us a couple of times but in the second half we set about them. We showed a lot more determination and within half an hour were 3–0 up. Any hopes they might have had of a repeat of the shock they pulled off at Ewood Park had vanished by then.

It was Andrei Kanchelskis's afternoon. His pace in the second half was too much for Scott Minto, the Charlton left-back, and he played a vital role in taking us through.

Our first goal showed the versatility of Mark Hughes, and the others came from Andrei's speed. We went ahead within 60 seconds of the restart as Mark smashed in a shot with his right foot after a Ryan Giggs corner. John Vaughan made a good save and the ball came back to Sparky who belted it home with his left. Our second came from a Charlton corner. Andrei picked up the clearance, raced half the length of the field and scored. Four minutes later the rout ended when he and Giggsy combined and Andrei finished things off, rolling the ball home.

With the Coca-Cola final a fortnight away we had reached the semi-final of the FA Cup and the next day learned our opponents would be Oldham. Joe Royle's fighters beat Bolton at Burnden Park. That was the game which took the live television spotlight away from us and it was a good win for Latics even though there was only one goal.

Neither Brian McClair nor I were used during the cup-tie but we both got on in the next game, which brought our biggest win of the season. Poor Trevor Francis. Once again he found himself playing the fall guy.

Brian McClair (No. 9) is besieged by Gary Pallister, Eric Cantona, Roy Keane and Paul Ince after scoring against Portsmouth in the 27th minute of our Coca-Cola Cup 5th-round replay at Fratton Park. The goal took us through to the semi-finals.
Empics/Steve Etherington

The incident which sparked off a major storm. Eric Cantona steps on the grounded John Moncur of Swindon and is sent off for his troubles. Three days later Eric got his marching orders again when we played Arsenal, and was banned for five games.
Action Images

Every picture tells a story. The Coca-Cola Cup Final was a far from happy time for me. Firstly I was unhappy at being left out of the side, then when we lost 3-1 to Aston Villa there was little to smile about. *Empics/Neal Simpson*

63 minutes have gone at Selhurst Park and the gaffer pulls me out of the action against Wimbledon. We lost the game 1-0 and with it the opportunity of increasing our lead at the top of the Premiership. Earlier that same day second-placed Blackburn were beaten 3-1 at Southampton. *Action Images*

The goal that probably changed our season. Mark Hughes (right) turns after smashing the ball into the Oldham net in the dying moments of extra time during the FA Cup semi-final at Wembley. Sparky is chased by the rest of us as Oldham's hopes sink out of sight. It was the boost our sagging form needed, the rest is history. *Action Images*

My 99th and final goal for United. Not the most spectacular – it went in off my stomach – but so valuable. This made it 3-1 in the FA Cup semi-final replay against Oldham and virtually made certain of our place at Wembley. *Empics/Paul Marriott*

Meet the Guv'nor! Paul Ince is first to grab me after I had scored against Oldham. The double was in sight and the celebrations had already started. *Action Images*

Leading out the team against Coventry City six days before the FA Cup Final; this was to be my final appearance for United. *Empics/Neal Simpson*

The Coventry game ended 0-0 and was more like a friendly than a serious Premiership encounter. *Action Images*

Champions Again!
For the second successive season we parade the Premiership trophy at Old Trafford. Paul Ince sports a new line in head gear (partly hidden, second left), and Clayton Blackmore (right) looks as though he's holding the television camera! *Action Images*

The victory parade. Banners wave and the fans cheer as we go on a lap of honour at Old Trafford following the presentation of the Premiership trophy. Can United make it three in a row? *Empics/Neal Simpson*

Singing in the rain. They're soaked to the skin, but who cares? Manchester United have done the double! The lads pose for the cameras after beating Chelsea 4-0 in the FA Cup Final. Club doctor Francis McKew, physio Jim McGregor (kneeling left) and Brian Kidd (right) somehow got into the picture as well. *Empics/Phil O'Brien*

That's all, folks. My days at United are over as I walk from the pitch following the FA Cup Final. After almost thirteen years with the club it is time for something new, but I have certainly been left with plenty of memories. *Empics/Phil O'Brien*

Twenty-four hours after winning the FA Cup the lads were on parade again, this time through the streets of Stretford where hundreds of thousands lined a triumphant route. There is no truth in the rumour that Pally asked them to cheer quietly because he had a hangover, but judging from this picture he was not alone! *Empics/Neal Simpson*

A view from the bench, but this time it is different. No longer the England player, I am looking forward to continuing my part-time post as assistant to Terry Venables. *Empics/Neal Simpson*

Here's to the future. The colours may be the same but this isn't Old Trafford. It's Ayrsome Park on the morning I was appointed player-manager of Middlesbrough. I am looking forward to the new challenge and hopefully will be able to bring success back to the club. *Empics/Paul Marriott*

Sheffield Wednesday thought they had seen the best of us in the Coca-Cola Cup semi-final, but when they found themselves 4–0 down at half-time in the League encounter at Old Trafford they must have wondered what they had done to deserve it. Ryan Giggs, Mark Hughes, Paul Ince and Eric Cantona inflicted the damage and Trevor looked shellshocked as we walked up the tunnel for the break.

The crowd were chanting 'We want five' and probably expected us to reach double figures, but we scored only once more in the second 45 minutes. The win boosted confidence, and our goal difference, and we knew that could prove vital.

Blackburn had a 15-day wait between games because their opponents were involved in the Cup, and we had re-established a 7-point lead by the time we went to the County Ground, Swindon, for our next Premiership fixture. We were top of the table on 71 points, Swindon were bottom with 25.

They had won just 4 games in their 34 league outings, compared with our 21, but anyone who thought they would be a pushover was wrong. They knew their chances of staying in the Premiership were slim, but they were determined they would go down fighting. We went ahead twice, they equalized twice and the game ended 2–2.

I wish that was all there was to it. The clash of top and bottom will not be remembered for the result but for an incident in the 65th minute when Eric Cantona and John Moncur chased the ball towards the touchline close on half-way. Moncur was pulling at Eric's shirt and you could see that he didn't like it. The Swindon man slid in and the two tangled for a moment, then as the ball broke free Eric stood on Moncur's chest.

It was described as 'stamping' in all the papers but that is not quite accurate. Eric used Moncur as a doorstep, pressing down with his foot as up went the balloon again. Out came the red card and off went our Eric to a two-match ban. He was the second United player to be sent off in three games, and our troubles had only just begun.

Three days later he was sent off again. This time it was at Highbury but I hope referee Vic Callow has since studied the video of the game against Arsenal, because I feel he slipped up.

Eric was dismissed for two bookable offences, both of which might have been waived by some referees. The first was for a challenge on Ian Selley and the second involved Tony Adams and Nigel Winterburn, and even Jimmy Hill thought the punishment was harsh!

Eric walked from the field in disgust and was banned for an additional three games – five matches in all. He was devastated, but dismissed all speculation that this would be the end of his days at Old Trafford. He got down to some hard work in training and added an extra half-hour to the time he devotes to signing autographs each day. Eric never refuses a polite request and goes out of his way to make sure that he disappoints nobody when the kids flock to The Cliff at half-term.

That is something that has to be seen to be believed. Some clubs would be pleased to attract as many people to their games as United get to watch them train when the schools are on holiday. Hundreds are allowed in and they cause quite a problem, even though they are only trying to be close to their heroes. With Ryan and Lee around it can be a bit like a pop concert at times and the club has to have stewards and police on duty to control things.

Eric is as good as gold. He will walk slowly along the front of the fans, who are pressed against the crush barriers which keep them away from our cars, signing all the time. When he gets to the end of the row, he will turn and go back again, and again and again. He shows amazing patience and I only wish those people who think that Eric Cantona is some sort of villain could see him with the supporters, they would certainly view things differently.

The suspension meant Eric would miss the game at Blackburn, the Premiership clash and semi-final against Oldham and the league matches against Leeds (away) and Wimbledon (away). He could not have chosen a more crucial time to be missing and you could almost see those who were waiting for us to slip rubbing their hands in glee.

Eric was available for the Coca-Cola Cup final which was our next game but the Cantona we saw at Wembley that afternoon was not the player we were used to. It could have had something to do with the suspension, but perhaps it was more to do with the way the opposition played.

Ron Atkinson had done his homework and stifled his supply of the ball. In doing so we found it difficult to get our passing game together. Even though we were without Peter Schmeichel we felt we had the players to beat Villa, but in the early stages we did not play well and went behind to a Dalian Atkinson goal.

I was watching things from the bench, a seat I was getting used to occupying, but this time I wore a collar and tie. Lee Sharpe had recovered from his hernia operation and won his way back into the side for the game at Arsenal, where he scored both goals. That earned him a substitute's place along with Brian McClair. Gary Walsh was the stand-by 'keeper as Les Sealey played his last game for the club.

Perhaps it was fitting that Les should go out in that way because it was at Wembley he really started his United career. That was back in 1990 when the boss decided to drop Jim Leighton for the replay of the FA Cup Final against Crystal Palace and handed the 'keeper's jersey to Les. What happened next is history and 'Lucky' Les had quite a time with us. He was in goal for the European Cup-Winners' Cup Final in Rotterdam and played with his knee heavily bandaged after being hurt in the League Cup Final a few weeks earlier.

Fate plunged him into another final against Aston Villa, the club he joined after leaving United on the arrival of Peter Schmeichel. Les thought he was surplus to requirements, signed for Ron Atkinson, and a season later was back with us saying: 'I wish I hadn't gone in the first place.' We went on to win the 1993 championship and Les was on the bench for the last four months of the season. Now there he was again taking centre stage for a big game.

Les's League Cup luck was out because he found himself losing to a Ron Atkinson side, just as he did in 1991 when Ron was in charge of Sheffield Wednesday. They beat us 1–0 that day, this time Villa won 3–1, but the scoreline was not a true reflection of the game.

We were never really in it for the first hour, then Lee Sharpe came on in place of Dion Dublin. He opened things up down the left and restored a bit of balance, but we went further behind when Dean Saunders scored in the 76th minute as he deflected a Richardson free kick past Les.

With 7 minutes to go Mark Hughes pulled us back when he shot from close range after Roy Keane had got in a good cross. We felt that if we could force extra time we could win because Villa were rocking. We threw caution to the wind and knew it could go wrong if we lost possession. Villa won the ball and broke out in the 90th minute. A shot came in and Andrei Kanchelskis, who had chased back to cover, blocked it on the goal-line with his hand.

It was a penalty and worse. Andrei became our fourth sending-off in five games.

I felt sorry for the lad and so did every other player on the pitch. The game was over when Dean Saunders stepped up to take the penalty and even if he had missed, the referee would have blown the final whistle before there had been another kick.

No-one blames Keith Cooper for showing Andrei the red card he had no alternative because he felt that it was deliberate hand-ball. He had to follow instructions and there had been a clamp-down by the Referees' Association because of complaints about a recent lack of consistency. Keith made his decision and stuck to it, but it must have been difficult for him at such a late stage of the game.

The treble chance gone, we still had double vision. We knew we had a difficult run-in to the end of the season, and things were being made harder for us by suspensions, but before our next game the pendulum seemed to swing our way.

Twenty-four hours before we were due to face Liverpool at Old Trafford, Blackburn were away to Wimbledon. They lost 4–1! That gave us a bit of breathing space because during our involvement with the Coca-Cola Cup Rovers had closed the gap to just 3 points and we both had 9 games left.

We knew a win against Liverpool would give us an advantage but we were also fully aware that the Merseysiders would be all out to stop us from retaining our title.

Again a referee found himself at the centre of things. This time it was the veteran Keith Hackett, who was in charge for his final game, while Liverpool manager Roy Evans enjoyed his first experience of selecting the side to face us.

Spirits had been a bit low immediately after Wembley and the boss shook things up a bit, dropping Ryan Giggs to substitute and bringing me in to join him on the bench while Lee Sharpe started his first senior game since December.

Peter Schmeichel was back in goal and we took the lead thanks to Paul Ince. His near-post header from a Sharpe cross turned out to be the match-winner.

Then came the controversy. Seventy minutes had gone when Liverpool broke down their left. The ball came into our penalty area and Andrei Kanchelskis and Michael Thomas jockeyed for possession. Thomas went down. Referee Hackett gave a penalty.

I had been on the field for 5 minutes after replacing Lee and had a good view of what had actually happened. Thankfully, so too had the linesman on our left. As the ball had been played towards them, Thomas was pulling at Andrei's shirt and using his elbow to unsettle him. He leaned into Andrei and the two of them fell backwards in a heap. It was a free kick to us and we knew it, and I am sure that so did most of the Liverpool players.

We pointed out the linesman's flag, Keith went across to consult him and changed his decision, awarding us the free kick. It took a brave man to do that sort of thing. He was admitting that he had made a mistake but he was big enough to be seen to put things right. Had he ignored the linesman, Liverpool might have scored from a penalty they should never have had. Some you win, some you lose.

Our lead was again 6 points, 8 games remained, and coming up next was the game everyone had been waiting for – Blackburn at Ewood Park. Five o'clock on Saturday 2 April and it was billed as the Premiership showdown.

Nothing went right for us. Rovers scored two great goals through Alan Shearer and won 2–0. The gauntlet had been taken up by Blackburn and it was obvious that they fancied their chances of winning the title.

The boss threw a wobbler when he learned that one of the things Kenny Dalglish had used to psyche up his players was cuttings of newspaper articles by some of our lads. He had pinned them to the walls of the temporary dressing-rooms Rovers were using while their new grandstand was being built and they were there for all to see.

It was a throw-back to those Ron Atkinson remarks of the previous season when he said we had lost our 'bottle.' That made us all the more determined, so the boss was furious that something similar had worked against us.

He slapped a ban not only on all interviews, but on all articles written by our players which appeared in all sorts of papers regularly throughout the season. 'This club will speak with one voice from now on,' he said. 'I will do the talking, the players will do the playing.'

Easter Saturday night was not a happy night in the United camp and we knew that the following week could also prove decisive. Our Easter Monday game was against Oldham and six days later we were due to face Latics again at Wembley.

It seems that nothing is simple in football nowadays. Traditionally the FA Cup semi-finals have been staged on a neutral ground within easy reach of the clubs involved, but recently there has been a trend to use Wembley. This started when Arsenal and Spurs were drawn against one another in 1991 and it was ideal for two big London clubs.

In 1993, when again one semi-final was an all-London affair, Sheffield Wednesday and Sheffield United insisted that they too be allowed to play each other at Wembley so that they were not disadvantaged. A year later The Football Association decided that Oldham and United would also use the stadium because the other semi-final, between Chelsea and Luton, was being held there.

That was understandable, it's only a few miles for the supporters to travel. But to ask two clubs from Greater Manchester to make a 400-mile round-trip was ludicrous.

Oldham wanted it, we certainly didn't. Latics saw it as a chance to give their fans a treat, while our supporters saw it as a rip-off!

United tried to help by subsidizing travel on the official coaches, where they charged half the normal fare, but ticket prices and the general cost of things at Wembley meant we were proving an expensive club to follow. It led to ill-feeling amongst the supporters when we had our dress rehearsal at Old Trafford, but there was no trouble – there never has been with Latics and hopefully never will be. The game was another of those which fell into the 'typical' category.

There was nothing typical about the first goal, though; in fact it was role-reversal time. Lee Sharpe made a good run down the left, found Steve Bruce and his cross was headed home by Ryan Giggs!

It stayed 1–0 until the 50th minute when Latics caught us with a break down their inside-left channel, Sean McCarthy hit a powerful left-foot shot and levelled the scores.

With Eric out for the second game of his suspension Brian McClair had started, but in the 63rd minute the boss replaced him with Dion Dublin, leaving me on the bench. Big Dion had only been on the field two minutes when his first real touch brought us a goal. It was a close-range shot from Giggsy's cross and it gave us the advantage we had been looking for. A minute later Paul Ince made it 3–1. Andrei Kanchelskis and Ryan Giggs used their speed to get clear of the Latics defence, which had come out to catch them offside, and they were joined by Incey. He finished the move with a tap amid cries for the linesman to disallow his effort.

You can never relax with Oldham, and with 20 minutes to go Graeme Sharp got their second. They made us hang on till the death for a 3–2 win.

Our lead at the top stayed at 3 points as Blackburn won 3–0 at Everton, and we knew they would have a psychological advantage over us a week later when we had no league game and they played Aston Villa at Ewood Park. If they won we would be top only on goal difference.

We had something else to occupy our thoughts and got ready for the semi-final. The boss told me that I would again be a substitute.

I felt that I had been in with a chance of starting the game because we had no fewer than three players suspended. Andrei was out because of his sending-off in the Coca-Cola final, Eric was on match three of his five-match ban, and Roy Keane was also banned for one game after picking up a booking on that fateful night at Highbury.

Three players suspended and one of them that night would find himself named PFA Player of the Year by his fellow professionals – Eric Cantona!

Big Dion's Premiership goal had earned him his place in the starting line-up and we played with Brian McClair in midfield along with Paul Ince and Lee Sharpe. Giggsy was on the right and Mark Hughes and Dion up front. Nicky Butt was named as the other outfield substitute and we looked on as Latics tried to prove that they could beat us on a big occasion.

In 1990 we also played them in the FA Cup semi-final, and it took two attempts to get through. It turned out to be a similar story in 1994.

The first 90 minutes were a bit ordinary. Both sides had chances but the game never really lived up to expectations and it went into extra time. The boss made our first switch after 73 minutes when he pushed me on in place of Dion. We got more of a grip in midfield but still could not get a goal, and when the last half-hour started we knew we would have a fight on our hands.

Things started to get a bit hectic as both sides realized how important it was to score. Three players were booked, Nicky Henry and Neil Pointon of Oldham and Paul Ince. We still had most of the possession but Oldham held out and a second game looked a certainty – although no-one expected the replay to come in such dramatic fashion.

The fans wanted a result and even though the Wembley attendance was 20,000 fewer than expected, there were 56,399 voices urging both sides on. Our supporters outnumbered Latics but the Oldham fans had something to shout about in the 106th minute when, just into the second half of extra time, Rick Holden took a corner. The ball fell to Neil Pointon and the full-back hit a powerful shot through our packed box. Peter couldn't reach it and it hit the back of the net.

The treble had gone, Blackburn were closing in, surely we couldn't let the lot slip through our fingers? You could sense the shuffling of feet on the terraces. Our supporters were worried, and we weren't exactly thrilled at the prospect.

The boss frantically signalled to Paul Parker and pulled him off. We had to attack and Nicky Butt came on giving us fresh legs at a vital moment. Was there enough time?

Mark Hughes was booked as the frustration mounted and we went on all-out assault. We had to get a goal but time was against us. The Oldham fans were whistling, urging the referee to end the game. Our supporters were preparing for the worst.

Pointon put the ball out of play on our right, level almost with the edge of the Latics' penalty area. The throw came in and I was involved in a passing move with Nicky Butt. He headed the ball towards the box, Brian McClair flicked it on and it fell in the path of Mark Hughes.

There were 45 seconds of extra time left and I cannot think of another player who could have handled the situation better than Mark. He was off balance, he was in a crowded box, he faced a packed goalmouth, yet he hit a volley of such power and accuracy it threatened to rip the Oldham net off its mountings.

That single shot meant so much and was possibly the most valuable goal Mark Hughes has ever scored although at that moment it meant just one thing. We were level and had forced a replay.

Firstly the goal brought an explosion of noise from our supporters. Hope was restored, it lifted our spirits sky-high and it totally deflated poor Oldham. They were stunned, shattered, flattened and as play restarted such was their condition that if time had allowed we could even have snatched a win. The fight had gone out of them but it would have been cruel for anyone to go out under such circumstances.

I was glad it ended the way it did. Glad? I was ecstatic!

I have had time to reflect on things since that afternoon and it is easy to imagine what might have happened had Mark not scored. We would have lost our chance of winning a second trophy. Leeds would have been eagerly waiting to play us three days later after having a long break to freshen up, and we could easily have found ourselves knocked off top spot in the League. The season could well have hung on that one shot.

The following night Blackburn beat Aston Villa in a poor game which showed that the tension was getting to them. We led the table only on goal difference with a game to spare.

Because of the replay the Leeds match was postponed and this meant that Eric Cantona's ban would end earlier. He would be available for the Manchester derby, while both Roy Keane and Andrei were clear for the second Oldham game.

The atmosphere at The Cliff on the morning after the semi-final was fantastic. You would have thought that we had actually gone the whole way and lifted the trophy the previous afternoon. I suppose in a way we did, but things were buzzing.

We had to prepare for a big game once again, but we knew that with those suspensions over we would be stronger. Oldham had their chance at Wembley and it had gone.

The replay was at Maine Road, where many people felt the original game should have been played, and when the boss finalized his line-up there was a name there I wanted to see – 'Robson.'

It was my first start since January and I was looking forward to it.

CHAPTER SIX

The Final Chapter

MY CAREER HAD TURNED FULL CIRCLE. AS I GOT READY FOR THE semi-final replay against Oldham I realized I was back where I had started, preparing to run out for a game at Maine Road, just as I had when I made my United début in October 1981. What I didn't know on that grey Wednesday evening was that this was to be my last appearance of any significance for the club.

Twelve and a half years earlier I took the field for my first Manchester derby, a goal-less draw against our local rivals which came a week after I had moved from West Bromwich Albion. Now another of our neighbours, Oldham, stood between us and a place in the FA Cup Final.

I knew we just had to get through – for United, for Sir Matt . . . and for me.

Although it had not been made public, I was already counting down the games before I would leave the club. Six Premiership fixtures and the FA Cup Final was all that remained. To bow out at Wembley would be the perfect ending to the final chapter of my Old Trafford story.

There had been a lot of speculation about my future, ranging from my taking up a coaching post with United to quitting the country to join Gary Lineker in Japan, but as the end of the season approached I had made up my mind.

Middlesbrough had officially approached United and asked the chairman and manager for permission to speak to me. They outlined their ideas for the future on Teesside and I liked what they had to say. I had already decided before the Oldham game that I would be heading for Ayrsome Park as player/manager, but until that time I still had a job to do for United and part of that included helping us to get to Wembley.

There was one major difference to that first appearance at Maine Road because we had been given the 'home' dressing-room and Latics were the 'away' team. As I walked out on to the field it felt as though we were playing at Old Trafford.

There were Reds everywhere.

Ticket sales had been slow for the second game but by kick-off time there didn't seem to be an empty seat anywhere, and as usual the majority holding belonged to United.

There was a tense atmosphere, which was only to be expected – the issue would be settled that night one way or another and both teams were fully aware of this. One club would finish up at Wembley, the other would become another statistic in the record books: 'losing semi-finalists 1994.'

From a personal viewpoint, I saw it as the chance to play in my fourth FA Cup Final and it was an opportunity I did not want to let slip. For the club, victory would mean our 10th Wembley final in the competition, the first being in 1948 when one of Sir Matt's teams won the Cup for the first time.

There had to be a winner. If the scores were level after extra time we would have a penalty shoot-out, and I don't think anyone in that 32,000 crowd wanted it to come to that, even if it meant their side getting through. Penalties are not the way to decide a major game, but until someone comes up with a better system that is how it has to be.

But you could forget penalties. We were going to win. Confidence flowed through the lads – not cockiness or complacency, just an overriding feeling that we were ready for the task ahead and determined to succeed. We could sense that no matter what Oldham had to offer we would win through.

The boss had made changes. Not only was I in the starting line-up, but Roy Keane and Andrei Kanchelskis were also included after their one-match suspensions. Lee Sharpe and Brian McClair were on the bench, with Dion Dublin dropping out of the fourteen.

We lined up with Andrei in his normal wide-right position, and Ryan returning to the left where he seems more at home, after being on the right-wing for most of the Wembley game.

Ryan has become recognized as a left-winger, but it may surprise some people to learn that he feels more at home playing as an out-and-out striker operating in the centre of the attack. That was his position when he caught the eye of the United steward Harold Wood, who pinched him from under the nose of Manchester City. Ryan was a United supporter, and Harold had watched his progress when he played for a kids' side close to his home.

He was eventually picked for Salford Schools and Harold was alarmed when City became interested. He persuaded the boss to have a look at him and the rest is history. Since he became one of the most popular players in the game today, City have claimed that they had him first, but there was no way that Giggsy would have signed for the Blues – well, not while Harold was around!

So Giggsy the striker is now a winger, but in the future, as he matures, he will probably move to that more central role, playing as he did with his school side, the club's junior teams and *England*! Yes, the Welsh Wizard played for England schoolboys, and not only that, he skippered the side.

Then he did the neatest of body swerves, changing not only his name but his nationality. When his parents separated Ryan Wilson became Ryan Giggs, as he took his mum's name. Then because he was born in Cardiff and was proud of the fact, he declared his loyalty to Wales and was selected for his first international by Terry Yorath. Even though he had lived virtually all his life in Salford, Giggsy was proud of his roots, much to England's regret.

He gets his leg pulled a lot by Lee Sharpe, who reckons that

Ryan made the switch because Sharpey would have kept him out of the England side. Whatever the reason it has certainly provided both nations with two outstanding left-sided players, and while Lee slipped into the background because of his injury problems last season, I expect to see him in contention for an international place again very soon.

We were back to something like our normal formation and as the game started Oldham's tactics became apparent. They tried to upset our pattern of play and we knew there would be a battle for midfield supremacy.

Mike Milligan and Nicky Henry did their usual harassing and a bit of overeagerness on our side led to Roy Keane being booked after only 5 minutes.

It was cut and thrust, but all the time I had the feeling it was going to be our night. Oldham's chance had come at Wembley . . . and gone.

They thought they were through and were gutted when Sparky equalized. The bottom fell out of their world at that moment and they showed it by the way they reacted after the final whistle.

We finished on such a high that it felt as if we had actually won the game. Latics' morale slumped, and from the moment our team coach pulled away from Wembley, we knew there was no way we were going to let them get on top for a second time.

The replay was 10 minutes old when we took the lead. I was involved in the build-up and finished by laying on the pass for Denis Irwin to get in a shot on goal. He made no mistake and the former Oldham man got his name on the scoresheet against his old club for the third time since his move across Manchester.

This had to be the most important goal of the three. His first two came in our 6–2 win at Boundary Park on Boxing Day 1991, and I'm sure that four years after his transfer Oldham still regret parting with Denis.

They had little alternative. In the summer of 1990 we were building for the future and it was difficult for Joe Royle to ignore the boss's offer, but I am sure United got the best part of the deal.

Denis had actually played against us the last time the clubs met in the FA Cup and that too was in a semi-final which went to a replay, with both matches staged at Maine Road. His performances in those games had a lot to do with United making a move for him, and what a player he has become since then. On that occasion we won at the second attempt so Denis knew what it felt like to be on the losing side at that stage of the competition, and none of us wanted to share the experience.

Apart from the fact that Latics were a Second Division side at that time, there was a strong similarity between their 1990 season and ours in 1994. They too had reached the League Cup Final and lost, but we had no intention of letting history repeat itself.

We were positive in our approach and we knew that Oldham must have had doubts before the game. Could any team truthfully say that they could give Manchester United a second chance and beat them?

The cheer which broke out as Denis scored summed up the feelings of our supporters. They knew the show was back on the road again and so did we. Our season had stuttered slightly and needed a lift: Sparkey's extra time goal had provided it. Would Denis's strike open the floodgates and add to the 22 goals we had now scored against them in the 8 meetings since they had won promotion?

Once we had gone out of the League Cup and the chance of winning the treble had disappeared, one or two of us had made it public knowledge that we wanted to complete the double for Sir Matt's memory. Our supporters were fully in favour and that possibly had something to do with the noise which followed that opening goal. They were also cheers of relief. We had gone through a tricky period in the games leading up to the semi-final.

Few clubs can go through a season without a slight slump in form, and with only two wins from six outings we knew we were in our tricky period. There were draws against Swindon and Arsenal, defeat in the League Cup Final and at Blackburn in the Premiership, and those wins against Liverpool and Latics were the only bright spots.

The draw at Wembley made it just two wins in seven games but when Sparky hit that late equalizer the overall feeling was that our luck had changed. Denis gave us another boost with his goal and 5 minutes later we struck again.

Andrei Kanchelskis did it all on his own this time, and it was a real stunner for Latics. He picked the ball up on the right wing and it looked as if he would make one of his usual breaks down to the goal-line. Instead he suddenly turned inside and ran across the pitch towards the left wing. Latics' defence chased to cover up the openings and fell back waiting for him to pass. Andrei held the ball, went further left, then turned towards goal and hit a powerful left-foot shot which eluded Jon Hallworth. We were 2–0 up.

The crowd rose to applaud the goal and we chased Andrei to offer our own congratulations. It was a special goal and could not have come at a better time. Latics were stunned but we knew that this would be the moment when they would have to make their biggest effort.

They came at us, we held out and went close again, before Oldham won a corner 5 minutes before half-time. Neil Pointon did it again. The former City full-back, playing on his old stomping ground, hit a shot through our defence just as he had at Wembley. It was 2–1 at the break.

As soon as the second half started Latics threw caution to the wind. They created a couple of openings but we stood firm as the frustration set in. Paul Bernard was booked in the 58th minute as we looked for goal number three – and guess who scored it?

Sixty-two minutes had gone. We won a corner on the right. As the cross came in, I ran towards goal. Steve Bruce went for the near post and I was looking for a flick on from him but I could not see the ball for all the bodies in the box.

Latics' goalkeeper Jon Hallworth went for it, misjudged his jump and at the last second I saw the chance. The ball was coming across the face of goal at an awkward height. It was too high to make good contact with my foot, and was dropping too low for a header unless I threw myself full-length and there wasn't space to do that. I just ran at it, hoping to force it home with my chest.

Even that was impossible as the ball bounced in the box but I managed to make contact with my thigh. I couldn't get any control and the ball shot off my leg and hit me full in the stomach and rebounded into the net!

That did it. We were 3–1 up and well on our way to the Cup Final, thanks to a goal I will never forget.

It was my 99th since joining United but I could hardly see it being looked upon as one of the goals of the season. Nor did I realize as we celebrated that it would turn out to be my last goal for the club – although I hope that everyone associated with United sees it as one of most important. The door to the double had opened a little wider.

The goal put the game further from Oldham's reach, and while it may not have been as spectacular as some of the previous 98 , I was still delighted to have scored it. A goal is a goal. Some may look better than others but they all count the same.

My mind went back to that semi-final in 1990 when I had scored my first goal against Latics. They had taken the lead through Earl Barrett after just 5 minutes and I got the equalizer thanks to a Neil Webb pass. It was the start of the good times. We went on to win the replay, then the FA Cup, and the trophies have poured in since then.

I have always enjoy playing against Oldham. There is something about their style which suits my game and I think that I can claim that I have never had a bad performance against them. Because of this it made it all the harder to take when the boss had left me out of the starters for the Wembley semi-final. We had players missing through suspension yet I was overlooked, and I felt that I had to show the gaffer he was wrong.

After coming on as substitute I had been involved in the move which led to Mark's equalizer. Now I had scored a crucial goal in the replay. If I had a point to prove, as far as I was concerned I had proved it.

We knew at 3–1 that the game was won. Oldham were finished, and five minutes later we definitely put the result beyond doubt. Giggsy scored after a confident run into the Latics' area. He pulled Jon Hallworth off his line, went sprinting beyond him and slotted the ball in off the inside of the far post from the narrowest of angles. While it was Ryan's 15th goal of the season it turned out to be the only one he scored in the FA Cup run.

The game finished 4–1, a scoreline which not only gave a clear indication of how we had performed on the night, but also of the determination we had all felt before the kick-off.

And who would we play in the Final? Why Chelsea, of course, the only side to have beaten us twice during the season, and only the second club to do that to us since Nottingham Forest in the campaign before the Premiership was launched.

It was the Final everyone had been hoping for, and I mean no disrespect to the beaten semi-finalists when I say that it provided a more attractive billing than Oldham against Luton. Their supporters would perhaps view things a little differently, but not the rest of football.

The Final was a month away, and in the period between that night at Maine Road and our fourth visit to Wembley in a season, lay the last half-dozen Premiership games. These would decide the destiny of the championship.

By now it was neck and neck in the league. We remained top but only on goal difference, although we still had a game more than Blackburn to play. Neither side could afford a slip, but both did.

There were 18 points to play for; six wins and no-one could touch us, and three days after the replay we were away to Wimbledon. It was a 5 p.m. kick-off, scheduled to start two hours after Blackburn had played Southampton at The Dell. By the time we had finished our pre-match warm up we knew exactly what we had to do.

It was almost a repeat of the previous season when we had faced Crystal Palace on that same ground as Blackburn beat Aston Villa at Ewood Park. That night's results had a major effect on the outcome of the 1993 championship. Could it be a similar story a year later?

Southampton were battling to stay up and their new manager Alan Ball had arrived at The Dell full of the enthusiasm he showed as a player. This rubbed off on the team he had inherited from Ian Branfoot and they clawed their way out of the relegation zone. They got themselves out of the bottom three, and at the same time, pulled off the shock of the season by beating Rovers in a game packed with excitement.

It also had the controversy of a disputed penalty which they still talk about in Blackburn. Iain Dowie and Paul Allen gave Saints a 2-0 lead, Stuart Ripley pulled one back for Rovers. Blackburn fought on, hoping for at least a draw, then the referee gave a dubious handball, awarded the spot kick to Southampton and Matt Le Tissier scored. It finished 3-1.

On the way to the game our supporters had listened to radio

commentary from The Dell, and we could sense their delight as they arrived at Selhurst Park. We knew that if we could beat Wimbledon, we would be 3 points clear as well as having the advantage of an extra game to play.

Unfortunately things do not always go according to plan. We lost.

It was hard to recognize us as the team that had played so well against Oldham. Our performance never reached anything like the standard we achieved three days earlier. The strain of those two big games showed through.

Wembley can drain players physically and mentally, and two semi-finals in three days was hardly the best way to prepare for 90 minutes against the Dons.

Wimbledon were fresh and eager to beat us in the same way that they had slammed Blackburn a fortnight earlier. There was no 4–1 against us, but they still took 6 home points from the two leaders. The party poopers had struck again!

We went down 1–0 and it was the only scoring chance Wimbledon had in the whole game. The goal came when Peter Schmeichel made a rare mistake. Twenty-two minutes had gone when Gary Elkins carried the ball down into the corner on our right. Peter came off his line anticipating the cross but leaving the near post uncovered. He probably expected a high ball aimed at the far side of his goal, but instead the cross was low and powerful.

Steve Bruce and Gary Pallister both came in to cover the move as John Fashanu bore down on goal. Peter caught the cross, but the ball shot out of his hands like a bar of soap in the shower and fell straight at the feet of Fash. Bang! One nil, and thank you very much!

I don't know what was going through Peter's mind at the time. He probably thought as he went for the ball that there would be boots flying. He seemed hesitant and uncertain, held back slightly and fumbled.

He was furious with himself and wasn't exactly flavour of the month with the boss afterwards, but he did what every top pro-fessional sportsman or woman must do when things go wrong. He took a good look at himself and got down to some extra hard work in training. He spent time going back to the basics of his game and working on every detail. That is the sign of a professional.

I am always surprised by those people who think that footballers simply roll up every day for a couple of hours training as preparation for a game. That sort of thing might have happened at some clubs in the past, but not today.

Players normally get one day off during a week, if they are lucky, and even then they will probably do some sort of training at home where most of us have fitness equipment. If we feel that a weakness has crept into our game we will put in added time at the training ground to correct it, turning to the coaching staff for advice and listening to what they have to say.

The same applies to every sport. The top people work hard to correct any technical errors they might be making. Can you imagine Linford Christie ignoring the advice of his coach if he spotted that the sprinter was losing vital time getting out of the starting blocks? Or Nick Faldo not bothering to work on his putting if his game slipped? No, they would work, work, work. And that is what footballers do.

It paid off for Peter, because after the Wimbledon upset he conceded just one more goal during the remainder of the season, although there is a lot more to the story than that as you will discover.

We stayed top despite losing and knew it was unlikely that either Newcastle or Arsenal would catch us as their games were running out. We had 5 to play, Blackburn 4, with the top of the Premiership showing the gap which had opened between second and third:

	P	W	D	L	F	A	PTS
Manchester United	37	23	10	4	72	37	79
Blackburn Rovers	38	24	7	7	59	32	79
Newcastle United	38	20	8	10	72	36	68
Arsenal	37	17	15	5	49	21	66

It was mathematically possible for Newcastle and Arsenal to catch the top two, but it would have meant both Blackburn and ourselves losing every game as they won all of theirs and that seemed highly unlikely. Reading the sports pages though, we sensed that people were still hoping we would slip up, and one of the teams who seemed to think they could upset our plans was none other than Manchester City.

Some of their players were happily telling everybody what they would or would not do to our championship dreams, with Terry Phelan possibly saying more than his fair share. I am told that he is actually a Red, who has supported United since he was a boy, but when he moved to Maine Road from Wimbledon he put it around that he was a Blue!

True or false it doesn't matter, but he found himself in hot water with his manager Brian Horton and apparently this was one of the reasons he was left out of the Old Trafford derby.

City had a player missing, we had one back. Remember Eric Cantona? His suspension was over. The prodigal son returned.

It was a typical derby. There was lots of noise from the United fans during the game but most of the shouting from the City contingent came before the kick-off – when they moaned about their ticket allocation – and afterwards, when they complained that both our goals were offside!

Catering for big games is difficult at Old Trafford because we could quite easily fill a much bigger stadium. The demand from United supporters has led to the club issuing extra tickets to people willing to pay in advance for the whole season, and has cut down the space for visiting fans. What should a club do. Turn away its own supporters on the off-chance that the visitors will bring 10,000, or sell the tickets to those who will definitely turn up? There is no argument.

We are seeing a change in football which actually is nothing more than a return to the early days. When travelling long distances to games was difficult, crowds were often made up of home supporters and a handful of visitors. It is only since the sixties that massive away followings have become the trend.

Clubs like Liverpool, Leeds and Newcastle have followed a similar plan to United's, and it is only those who cannot fill their grounds regularly who welcome large numbers of away supporters. Perhaps in the future we will see games watched only by the home fans, as the visitors show the action on giant screens back at their own ground. Certainly United have tried this and it works, but I hope that away support doesn't fade out completely.

The away fans at Old Trafford had little to cheer in the derby as we won 2–0. Eric scored twice and neither goal was questioned by the officials. He took his personal tally to 22 for the season and the win reopened that 3-point gap.

City played well, their performance being a possible indication that the threat of relegation which had haunted them for months, had more or less disappeared. It also showed how they had got themselves out of trouble, thanks to the purchase of players like Uwe Rossler and Paul Walsh who both put in good performances.

City attacked well, but in defence they could not handle the pace of Andrei Kanchelskis and the skills of Mark Hughes and Eric Cantona. They might have claimed that they felt hard done by as far as the goals were concerned, but we could quite easily have had two or three more.

Knowing that the Blues had secured their place in the Premier-ship for another season at least kept one section of Manchester happy, but the other expected a little more from life than that. The win meant we could finish no lower than second place and that we had qualified for the UEFA Cup. Newcastle and Arsenal were out of the race. Later we would also qualify for the Cup-Winners' Cup, then the Champions' Cup. Not many teams have done that.

We had played 38 games, Blackburn were due to play their 39th when they met QPR at Ewood Park the following day. It was now a two-horse race, and as they came into the closing few furlongs Blackburn stumbled yet again. They drew 1–1 with Rangers.

There was all the usual claptrap about them 'losing their bottle', most of it appearing on the pages of certain papers, but we knew that the lads at Ewood Park would take as much notice of that sort of rubbish as we did. Players don't lose games because they have lost their nerve – they go down because the opposition has either played better or had some of the luck which might have been going. Sometimes both.

Rovers had three matches left, away to West Ham and Coventry, and their final fixture at home to Ipswich. Earlier in the season they had been beaten at Ewood Park by The Hammers and at

Portman Road by Ipswich, so we knew that they would not exactly have everything their own way.

Our last three games were the trip to Ipswich, followed by home clashes with Southampton, who were still fighting to stay up, and Coventry.

Before that we had a crucial away game – at Leeds. It followed 4 days after the derby and I spent the whole 90 minutes on the subs' bench, as I had against City.

For once I was a willing spectator because I am sure no-one would argue with me when I say I witnessed our best performance of the season. What a time to turn it on, as Blackburn were winning away to West Ham.

The lads were outstanding and to do it at a ground like Elland Road, where we are never given the friendliest of receptions by the Leeds supporters, made it an even greater achievement. I think the hostility of the Leeds fans was in the boss's mind when he decided that we would get to the ground earlier than usual.

The previous season there had been an unofficial reception committee waiting for Eric Cantona as he returned to Elland Road for his first game against the club which sold him to us. It was pretty unpleasant stepping from the coach to be spat upon and hit by torrents of abuse from fans crowded round the players' entrance. I am sure that if the same thing happened to players arriving at Old Trafford some serious action would be taken, and I cannot believe that the police allow them to get away with it.

Fergie's plan worked. This time it was much quieter. We were inside before many folk realized and relaxing in the dressing-rooms as the Leeds fans saved their venom for the game.

In the opening stages Leeds tried hard to upset our rhythm but we felt under no pressure, and even though we went off at half-time without a goal being scored by either side, we had created the better chances.

The second 45 minutes were totally one-sided. Three minutes after the restart Andrei Kanchelskis struck a goal created by the quick thinking of Mark Hughes. He carried the ball across the front of the Leeds penalty area, then found Andrei running into yards of space. The strike was swift and incisive, and even though we had been playing well up to that point, the lads seemed to step up a gear. We controlled the game and silenced the crowd's hatred.

It seemed that it would only be a matter of time before we got another, and Elland Road was a strangely quiet place as the home fans saw their favourites fighting to survive against the club they like the least. Six minutes from time Sparky did it again. He beat a defender and slipped the ball into an opening for Ryan to run on to and he made no mistake.

Two–nil, and I felt sorry for the hundreds, possibly thousands, of Leeds fans who missed such a good goal because they had gone home earlier than planned.

It was an important win. Blackburn had beaten West Ham 2–1 so the gap stayed at 2 points.

Just before we left Elland Road I received a message to ring Terry Venables the next morning. Earlier that day he had been guest speaker at a lunch organized by the Manchester Branch of the Football Writers' Association. He had outlined his England plans to the press and I was flattered to learn how much they involved me.

'I would like to bring someone along who eventually will take over from me, and I would think that Bryan would be one of the people who fall into that category,' Terry had said. Hopefully that is a prediction which may come true one day, and when I rang him the next morning he asked me about my feelings on joining his staff on a full-time basis.

It wasn't a take-it-or-leave-it offer, but an invitation to work alongside him if I wanted to. I had to say no. If I accepted the job and had gone with Terry it would have meant me giving up too many things at once.

Firstly I would have been forced to quit as a player, and I wanted at least one more season. I would also have lost the everyday involvement with a club, and after twenty-two years that would have been a terrific wrench. There is a certain camaraderie which builds up when you spend each daytime working towards the next objective.

Training sessions, especially under someone like Brian Kidd, Alex's assistant at Old Trafford, can be enjoyable even for someone who has been in the game as long as I have, and I wanted to sample this as a manager rather than just be part of the international set-up, which is totally different.

Terry told me that my decision would not affect my part-time role, but he has perhaps set my next target. As player-manager with Middlesbrough I know I can gradually ease my way from one half of the job into the other.

The transition from player to manager will be gradual and when I eventually hang up my boots I will know that I did what I intended to do, and continued as a player for as long as possible. I have often said that the time to give up playing is when you no longer enjoy it, but I think that age will also have a part to play. I cannot see the time when I might not enjoy a game, but unfortunately there are few 65-year-olds playing at top level!

My plan is to ease into management and hopefully by that time I will have learned enough to keep me secure in the job. As for ambitions, if the day was to come when I was offered the England job then I would seriously consider it, provided I was satisfied that I had proved myself as a club manager.

There is also speculation that one day I might return to Old Trafford, and I was delighted to hear Martin Edwards predicting that perhaps one day I could be back.

The closing games of the season were going to provide plenty of excitement and Sky Television called the tune as far as the fixture list was concerned. They knew there would be an audience hungry to see the outcome of the Premiership and screened games accordingly.

We were away to Ipswich on Sunday 1 May, while Blackburn travelled to Coventry the following evening for their penultimate match. Both fixtures were watched by massive satellite audiences.

As far as records go, our performances against Ipswich since they came back to the top flight had been nothing to write home about. We had played them three times, lost once and drawn twice, and there was every reason to believe that the television planners might be right. An upset could be on the cards.

Ipswich were fighting to survive in the Premiership and if they did at the expense of the big boys then that would make the story all the more intriguing. The game at Portman Road did provide some added drama to the closing stages of the season, but nobody could have predicted the way that it came.

Lee Sharpe was back in the squad and I was left out, even

though I hadn't put a foot wrong in my two previous matches! Paul Ince was having problems with a slight groin strain and had been doubtful since the morning after the Leeds game. Because of this I half expected to be included.

The boss had other ideas. For the third successive game Gary Walsh was on the bench along with Brian McClair and Lee, and it was our stand-by goalkeeper who found himself playing a leading role in the televised thriller.

Ipswich were prepared to fight all the way. They had to, relegation stared them in the face after a remarkable slump in form. They needed something from their last two games and could not have chosen more difficult opponents if they had tried. After facing us that afternoon, their last game of the season was away to Blackburn six or seven days later.

Six or seven? The date hinged on results that weekend. If the championship was still in the balance their game against Blackburn would be switched to the Sunday, the day we played Coventry at Old Trafford. If not, it would be played on a normal Saturday afternoon. The clubs involved in the relegation tussle complained that Ipswich could have an unfair advantage if they played at a different time from them, but the game was still scheduled for the following Sunday if necessary.

Ipswich's record building up to our visit had been far from impressive. They had taken just 6 points from 11 matches, a win over Aston Villa and three draws. Seven defeats had plunged them from 13th place in February to the brink of the drop.

There was no way they were going to let us walk in and take three points, and after withstanding our early efforts they scored first through Chris Kiwomya, the player who had done the same against us the previous season. The goal came after Ian Marshall fired in a fairly weak shot which should have been no problem for Peter Schmeichel. However, the ball bobbled on the topsoil which had been spread in the well-scarred goalmouth and he could not hold it. He was fooled both by the lack of strength in the shot and the way the ball came at him. It flew out of his grasp straight to Kiwomya who was coming in fast.

Then came the drama. Ten minutes later, as we fought to get level, the same two players were involved in a clash at the edge of the box.

Kiwomya came in feet first as Peter tried to kick the ball clear and the big Dane fell to the ground in agony as his foot made contact with the sole of the Ipswich striker's boot. He was helped off with damaged ankle ligaments and Gary Walsh took over.

What more did the television audience want? The defending champions were a goal down, had lost their goalkeeper, and had called in a player who had not made a league appearance for two years. You could almost hear them cheering in Blackburn.

Any celebrations were premature. We reorganized and, with Walshy's confidence growing by the second, were level within 6 minutes.

It was that man Cantona again, popping up to score a valuable goal after a good run down the right and a perfect cross from Andrei Kanchelskis.

We went off 1–1 and 2 minutes into the second period took the lead. We won a throw in. Roy Keane got himself into a good position, crossed, and Ryan Giggs gave us victory with a close-range shot.

The following night Coventry beat Blackburn 2–1 at Highfield Road. We were back where our story started – champions again and time for Steve Bruce to host yet another party.

The television audience saw not only the high-speed performance by Coventry, who fully deserved their three points, but were taken through the keyhole into Chez Bruce, where Steve had been joined by Peter Schmeichel and Paul Parker for their after-match comments. Steve revealed that he had missed some of the Coventry game because he had been out to buy some extra champagne, but the truth is that he couldn't bear to watch.

We were on the verge of taking our second successive title and it got to him. He wasn't alone. Roy Keane later revealed that he spent the whole 90 minutes in his bedroom listening to his compact disc player.

A year earlier the gaffer played golf rather than watch that crucial Villa versus Oldham game, and we all thought he was being cool!

We were champions again. It was incredible. We had led from the front for virtually the whole season and in the end had the staying power to hold off that unexpected challenge from Kenny Dalglish's team. We admired the way that Blackburn fought to overtake us and they deserved their European place for finishing second. I know that next season the lads will expect a similar challenge.

The long road through 42 games was not yet over but there was now no way we could be caught, and our remaining matches against Southampton and Coventry became a formality.

We beat Southampton 2–0 but even so they still managed to stay in the Premiership, as Swindon, Oldham and Sheffield United were relegated. The game against Coventry was a total anti-climax.

As soon as the destiny of the championship was known plans were announced that surprised many people. Instead of being presented with the Premiership Trophy on Wednesday 4 May, our first game after we became champions, we were told it would be handed over the following Sunday.

Why not the Wednesday? Because the Sunday game was on television.

The decision meant that the 44,705 fans who turned up to celebrate our second successive title watched a highly competitive game of football against a battling Southampton, but some of them missed out on the championship presentation. They saw Andrei and Sparky score, while the trophy had an extra polish after being taken from its display cabinet in our museum.

Then on the Sunday a crowd of just twelve more spectators – plus the television viewers – saw a hardly recognizable United side draw 0–0 against Coventry in a fixture which was treated more like a friendly than a serious Premiership game.

Before the match the gaffer made public my plans for the future and announced that it would be my last appearance at Old Trafford. I had expected it, of course, but at that time did not reveal anything about my decision to move to Middlesbrough.

That would have been unfair. I was still a Manchester United player and ready to give 100 per cent in any games I played for them. The Coventry match may have been my last home fixture but I hoped for a little bit more.

I wanted to end my United career by being part of the squad six days later when we were to face Chelsea at Wembley. Could there be a more fitting finale?

The announcement about Middlesbrough would have to wait, although the sports writers still tried to predict where I would end up. There had been approaches from two Premiership clubs and it was easy to guess which ones. I made no secret about my friendship with Trevor Francis, at Sheffield Wednesday, and Ron Atkinson would have liked me to end my playing days with him.

Considering our links at West Brom and Old Trafford, joining Ron at Aston Villa would have been quite fitting. But it was something I could not do. My feelings for United were such that I would not even consider the thought of playing against them in a Premiership game the following season.

It would not have been right, although fate is such that I will probably have a bet on a United v. Middlesbrough cup-tie coming up soon, and who knows I might still be playing when 'Boro reach the top flight.

So because of the boss's announcement, there was an extra presentation before the Coventry game. Denis Law handed me an award from Carling for my services to the game. But I wanted to get my hands on something else before I said goodbye to Old Trafford. I dearly wanted another FA Cup winners' medal.

I know that I have three already, and it was a great honour to collect the cup in 1983, 1985 and 1990. I also thought it was a terrific gesture by Steve Bruce when he insisted that I went up with him to collect the championship trophy at the end of that afternoon's match, just as we had done a season earlier. But I hoped for one more honour.

Manchester United were on course for the double. One half – the most difficult – had been achieved. The other, which had slipped through the fingers of Sir Matt the last time the club had been close in 1957, was six days away.

We reported for training the morning after that closing Premiership game, in which Alex had fielded a side including Gary Neville and Colin McKee, two boys who will figure in the story of the future, and I still felt I was in with a chance of playing in the final.

The days passed by and eventually I was told that I was not going to be part of the gaffer's plans. I felt let down.

The boss had disappointed me badly when he left me out of the Coca-Cola Cup Final, but this was an even bigger blow. Before the Coca-Cola game he had said that the players who had got the club to Wembley would play in the final. I had been involved in every round but the semi-final, and even then I was on the bench for the second leg, and thought I had done enough to be included. I was the one who was left out and it hurt.

To be left out a second time was devastating. I thought that my performance after coming on as substitute during the first semi-final at Wembley, then the way I had played in the replay, plus that goal, had been enough to justify my selection. Even if it was only a seat on the sub's bench I had hoped to be involved, but it was not to be.

I know what was in the boss's mind. Lee Sharpe is a young player with a long way to go in his career. He has a five-year contract, Brian McClair has signed a three-year deal, I was leaving. So who does he have to keep happy?

Not me.

My claim for a place had nothing to do with sentiment. I felt that I had shown by my performances that I deserved to be included and it would have been such a fitting end to my United career if I could have had the chance of playing in the last few minutes of the final, as Brian McClair did, and perhaps score that 100th goal. That would have been terrific.

There was nothing I could do. The boss named his side and that was that. We did not fall out, there was no row. There was little point in anything like that, the manager had made his decision and I had to abide by it.

On the day of the final I joined in everything that went on. Before the game I spoke to the media and told them of my disappointment but I also went round the dressing-room and did all that I could to get the lads in the right frame of mind for the game. I did all my usual things, chatting to them and encouraging them, then took my seat behind the substitutes to watch the game.

Right from the start Chelsea showed that they were out to stop us from achieving the double and would resort to anything to do so. They were very lucky not to have a player sent off as early as the second minute when Erland Johnsen up-ended Ryan Giggs as he ran at their penalty area. Giggsy almost did a cartwheel as the Norwegian came in with no intention of playing the ball. It was no surprise when he had his name taken by David Elleray.

My mind flashed back to 1985. That challenge was far worse than

Kevin Moran's tackle on Peter Reid, yet big Kev made history by becoming the first player to be sent off in an FA Cup Final. I didn't wish anything on Johnsen but he was a very fortunate chap. You need luck to win cups. Was this going to be Chelsea's day?

Peter Schmeichel was back in goal for us having declared himself fit shortly after the Coventry match and he was tested a couple of times before Chelsea had their best chance of the half. It fell to none other than Gavin Peacock, but his chip bounced off our crossbar in the 26th minute, and although we were playing well below par we managed to hold out till half-time without conceding a goal.

You need luck to win cups.

The rain was belting down and my Cup Final suit got a soaking as we made the dash between the dressing-room and the part shelter of the touchline seats below the Royal Box. Half-time was hectic. The lads had to get their passing going, Chelsea were outnumbering us in midfield, I was desparate to get on. But . . .

The second half was a total contrast to the first and that bit of fire the boss demanded at the break started to show. A lot had been made of the fact that the pressure was off both sides before the game because each had secured its European place. As the champions we were back in the big one, and even if we did the double Chelsea would qualify for the Cup-Winners' Cup. There was only the FA cup to play for, but it seemed that we were too relaxed.

Slowly we began to turn things round. Denis Irwin had a good free kick saved, and then just on the hour he and Ryan Giggs combined in a run down the left.

The ball was played into Denis's feet and as he went for goal he was brought down by Eddie Newton. Penalty! We all leapt from our seats and stayed on our feet as Eric tucked the ball into the corner of Kharine's net.

Five minutes later Eric, who had been blocked out of things in the first half, scored his second with an identical penalty. This time it came when Andrei Kanchelskis was fouled by Frank Sinclair as he went full speed for the Chelsea box. It was a borderline decision but Eric wasn't bothered about detail, he slotted the ball to Kharine's left as he again went right, and we were on our way.

Two minutes later poor Sinclair boobed on the edge of his box, Mark Hughes pounced, and struck his fourth Wembley goal in as many appearances that season. Then as the end approached the boss gave the signal to use his two substitutes. Brian and Lee had warmed up and now they replaced Denis and Andrei and I didn't know whether to laugh or cry.

Brian slotted home number 4 with virtually his first touch after Paul Ince had made a superb run through the middle, and the whistle went. I joined in the celebrations, but at the back of my mind there was always the thought that it could have been me out there for that last five minutes.

I am not being selfish, I do not begrudge any of my mates their moment of glory, and who knows what might have happened if I had been involved. It was a personal disappointment but a great achievement by the club and that is what must come first. I would rather not have played and seen us win than to have been on the losing side.

The lads went up and collected the cup, and I knew just how they felt as I watched them take the cheers and have a quiet peep at their medals. I had done it before, and there is nothing to compare with the emotion and pride. That is why I turned down the club's offer of a specially-struck medal. They were ready to ask the Football Association to make one just for me, but it would have been meaningless. If you are not on the team sheet, why should you want a medal?

I found it hard to hide my disappointment but afterwards realized that it must have been a difficult time for the manager. He had made a similar decision in 1990 when he left Jim Leighton out for the replay against Crystal Palace and Les Sealey helped us win the FA Cup that year. This time he had to overlook me and stick with the players who would be with him for the next campaign.

I went to the club's celebration dinner that night, then the next day reported to Bisham Abbey for England's preparations for the two friendlies we were playing against Greece and Norway, countries who were going to America for the World Cup while we stayed at home.

The lads went back to Manchester to parade through the streets on the open-topped bus with their two trophies and, unlike the previous year when the rain never stopped, the only soaking they took was from the inside!

The long season was over. It had perhaps ended on a low note as far as I was concerned, but back in Manchester they had plenty to sing about, and when I look back on my career with United I have thousands of happy moments to outweigh that little disappointment at the end.

For the first time in the club's history we had done the double and I was delighted to have been part of that. We were only the fourth club this century to lift both the league championship and the FA Cup in the same season and that will be a lasting memory for me.

We did the double for Sir Matt, for Manchester United and for our supporters, and it was a great thrill to be able to call ourselves . . . Champions Again!

FA Carling Premiership 1993–94

		P	W	D	L	F	A	PTS
1	Man. United	42	27	11	4	80	38	92
2	Blackburn	42	25	9	8	63	36	84
3	Newcastle Utd	42	23	8	11	82	41	77
4	Arsenal	42	18	17	7	53	28	71
5	Leeds Utd	42	18	16	8	65	39	70
6	Wimbledon	42	18	11	13	56	53	65
7	Sheff. Wed.	42	16	16	10	76	54	64
8	Liverpool	42	17	9	16	59	55	60
9	QPR	42	16	12	14	62	61	60
10	Aston Villa	42	15	12	15	46	50	57
11	Coventry	42	14	14	14	43	45	56
12	Norwich City	42	12	17	13	65	61	53
13	West Ham Utd	42	13	13	16	47	58	52
14	Chelsea	42	13	12	17	49	53	51
15	Tottenham H.	42	11	12	19	54	59	45
16	Man. City	42	9	18	15	38	49	45

		P	W	D	L	F	A	PTS
17	Everton	42	12	8	22	42	63	44
18	Southampton	42	12	7	23	49	66	43
19	Ipswich	42	9	16	17	35	58	43
20	Sheff. Utd	42	8	18	16	42	60	42
21	Oldham A.	42	9	13	20	42	68	40
22	Swindon T.	42	5	15	22	47	100	30

MATCH DETAILS

7 Aug.	FA CHARITY SHIELD, WEMBLEY STADIUM	66,519

Manchester United (1) 1	**Arsenal (1) 1**
Hughes (8)	**Wright (40)**
(United won 5–4 on penalties)	

MANCHESTER UNITED: Schmeichel, Parker, Irwin, Bruce, Kanchelskis, Pallister, Cantona, Ince, Keane, Hughes, Giggs.
SUBS: Robson (for Giggs), McClair, Sharpe, Ferguson, Sealey.

ARSENAL: Seaman, Dixon, Winterburn, Davis, Linighan, Adams, Campbell, Wright, Merson, Limpar, Jensen.
SUBS: Keown (for Dixon), McGoldrick (for Limpar), Selley, Heaney, Miller.

Two superb goals were the highlights of this game but in the end the destiny of the Charity Shield was decided by a penalty shoot-out, with big Peter making an important save against his opposite number Dave Seaman.

| 15 Aug. | FA CARLING PREMIERSHIP | CARROW ROAD | 19,705 |

| Norwich City (0) 0 | Manchester United (1) 2
Giggs (25)
Robson (57) |

NORWICH: Gunn, Culverhouse, Butterworth, Polston, Newman, Bowen, Crook, Goss, Fox, Sutton, Robins.
SUBS: Ekoku (for Robins), Megson, Howie.

MANCHESTER UNITED: Schmeichel, Parker, Irwin, Bruce, Kanchelskis, Pallister, Robson, Ince, Keane, Hughes, Giggs.
SUBS: Sharpe, McClair, Sealey.

Mike Walker's tactics surprised everyone, including the home fans, with Norwich playing a defensive formation. It backfired as the youngest and oldest members of the side managed to get on to the score-sheet. Mark Hughes had an outstanding game and it was the perfect start to the new season.

P	W	D	L	F	A	PTS	PSN
1	1	0	0	2	0	3	–

| 18 Aug. | FA CARLING PREMIERSHIP | OLD TRAFFORD | 41,949 |

| Manchester United (2) 3
Keane (17, 44)
Hughes (86) | Sheffield United (0) 0 |

MANCHESTER UNITED: Schmeichel, Parker, Irwin, Bruce, Kanchelskis, Pallister, Robson, Ince, Keane, Hughes, Giggs.
SUBS: Sharpe, McClair (for Robson), Sealey.

SHEFFIELD UNITED: Kelly, Hoyland, Cowan, Pemberton, Rogers, Falconer, Bradshaw, Tuttle, Scott, Whitehouse, Ward.
SUBS: Gage (for Rogers), Cork (for Hoyland), Tracey.

Sheffield tried to outfox us with Jamie Hoyland playing sweeper, but once Roy Keane had scored the opening goal the Blades had no answer and we ran out easy winners.

P	W	D	L	F	A	PTS	PSN
2	2	0	0	5	0	6	1

| 21 Aug. | FA CARLING PREMIERSHIP | OLD TRAFFORD | 41,829 |

Manchester United (1) 1	Newcastle United (0) 1
Giggs (40)	Cole (70)

MANCHESTER UNITED: Schmeichel, Parker, Irwin, Bruce, Kanchelskis, Pallister, Robson, Ince, Keane, Hughes, Giggs.
SUBS: Sharpe (for Parker), McClair (for Kanchelskis), Sealey.

NEWCASTLE UNITED: Srnicek, Venison, Watson, Scott, Beresford, Clark, Lee, Bracewell, Papavasiliou, Cole, O'Brien.
SUBS: Allen, Wright, Appleby.

Ryan Giggs got his second of the season and Andy Cole his first – and there turned out to be many more to come for the Newcastle striker. Both sets of supporters enjoyed this one because Newcastle played attacking football and deserved their point, their first of the season.

P	W	D	L	F	A	PTS	PSN
3	2	1	0	6	1	7	4

| 23 Aug. | FA CARLING PREMIERSHIP | VILLA PARK | 39,624 |

Aston Villa (1) 1	Manchester United (1) 2
Atkinson (45)	Sharpe (17, 74)

ASTON VILLA: Spink, Barrett, Staunton, Teale, McGrath, Richardson, Houghton, Parker, Saunders, Atkinson, Small.
SUBS: Froggatt (for Staunton), Whittingham (for Houghton), Bosnich.

MANCHESTER UNITED: Schmeichel, Parker, Irwin, Bruce, Sharpe, Pallister, Kanchelskis, Ince, Keane, Hughes, Giggs.
SUBS: McClair, Ferguson, Sealey.

Lee Sharpe scored two terrific goals against the club he supported when he was a boy. It was a tremendous game, with both sides playing fast flowing football, and we showed everyone why we had taken the championship the previous season.

P	W	D	L	F	A	PTS	PSN
4	3	1	0	8	2	10	1

| 28 Aug. | FA CARLING PREMIERSHIP | THE DELL | 16,189 |

Southampton (1) 1	Manchester United (2) 3
Maddison (12)	Sharpe (5), Cantona (15)
	Irwin (48)

SOUTHAMPTON: Flowers, Kenna, Adams, Moore, Bartlett, Monkou, Le Tissier, Cockerill, Dowie, Maddison, Benali.
SUBS: Banger (for Cockerill), Charlton (for Moore), Andrews.

MANCHESTER UNITED: Schmeichel, Parker, Irwin, Bruce, Sharpe, Pallister, Cantona, Ince, Keane, Hughes, Giggs.
SUBS: McClair (for Giggs), Kanchelskis (for Keane), Sealey.

Sharpey was at it again but this was Eric's comeback day and he put on a special show. The French superstar controlled the game and scored a super goal into the bargain. Tim Flowers was in fine form and probably boosted his transfer price before Kenny Dalglish made the swoop which took him to Blackburn.

P	W	D	L	F	A	PTS	PSN
5	4	1	0	11	3	13	1

1 Sept.	FA CARLING PREMIERSHIP	OLD TRAFFORD	44,613

Manchester United (2) 3 Sharpe (7), Cantona (44 pen) Bruce (88)	**West Ham United (0) 0**

MANCHESTER UNITED: Schmeichel, Parker, Irwin, Bruce, Sharpe, Pallister, Cantona, Ince, Keane, Kanchelskis, Giggs.
SUBS: McClair (for Ince), Robson (for Kanchelskis), Sealey.

WEST HAM: Miklosko, Breacker, Dicks, Potts, Foster, M. Allen, Rowland, Holmes, Morley, C. Allen, Gordon.
SUBS: Gayle (for M. Allen), M. Robson (for Gordon), Peyton.

Brucie's face was a picture when Eric picked up the ball and took the penalty. He thought he was our offical spot kicker! Steve still managed to get on the score-sheet with a little near-post header just before time but Lee Sharpe had another good game and certainly found the form he had been producing before his illness.

P	W	D	L	F	A	PTS	PSN
6	5	1	0	14	3	16	1

11 Sept.	FA CARLING PREMIERSHIP	STAMFORD BRIDGE	37,064

Chelsea (1) 1 Peacock (17)	**Manchester United (0) 0**

CHELSEA: Kharine, Clarke, Donaghy, Dow, Kjeldbjerg, Hoddle, Sinclair, Newton, Cascarino, Peacock, Wise.
SUBS: Shipperley (for Cascarino), Hall (for Dow), Hitchcock.

MANCHESTER UNITED: Schmeichel, Parker, Irwin, Bruce, Sharpe, Pallister, Cantona, Ince, Keane, Robson, Giggs.
SUBS: McClair (for Robson), Kanchelskis, Sealey.

No Sparkey and no spark. Not the best of performances but any luck that was going went Chelsea's way, especially when Eric Cantona tried to lob Kharine from close to the half-way line and the ball bounced onto the Chelsea crossbar. Gavin Peacock got the winner and we went down for the first time since March.

P	W	D	L	F	A	PTS	PSN
7	5	1	1	14	4	16	1

---

15 Sept.   EUROPEAN CUP FIRST ROUND (1) BUDAPEST   9,000

Honved (1) 2	Manchester United (3) 3
Szabados (40)	Keane (8, 42)
Stefanov (68)	Cantona (44)

HONVED: Brockhauser, Szabados, Plokai, Halmai, Banfi, Csehi, Illes, Stefanov, Duro, Vincze, Hamar.
SUBS: Orosz (for Duro), Salloi, Dragoner, Toth, Rott.

MANCHESTER UNITED: Schmeichel, Parker, Irwin, Bruce, Sharpe, Pallister, Robson, Ince, Cantona, Keane, Giggs.
SUBS: Phelan (for Giggs), Martin, Dublin, Butt, Sealey.

The club's first step into the European Champions' Cup for 25 years and a great start, with Roy Keane stunning the Hungarians early in the game. Honved fought back but two goals just before half-time put the tie safely in our hands and confidence was high that we would get through to the second round.

---

19 Sept.   FA CARLING PREMIERSHIP   OLD TRAFFORD   44,009

Manchester United (1) 1	Arsenal (0) 0
Cantona (37)	

MANCHESTER UNITED: Schmeichel, Parker, Irwin, Bruce, Sharpe, Pallister, Cantona, Ince, Keane, Hughes, Giggs.
SUBS: McClair (for Hughes), Kanchelskis, Sealey.

ARSENAL: Seaman, Keown, Linighan, Adams, Winterburn, Mc-Goldrick, Jensen, Merson, Hillier, Campbell, Wright.
SUBS: Davis (for Hillier), Smith (for Merson), Miller.

No penalty shoot-out this time but there was a terrific strike from a free kick by Eric Cantona. Paul Ince rolled the ball towards him and he bent it beyond Dave Seaman to give us maxiumum points and keep up our challenge at the top. The win helped us to open a three point gap over Arsenal.

P	W	D	L	F	A	PTS	PSN
8	6	1	1	15	4	19	1

---

22 Sept.   **COCA-COLA CUP SECOND ROUND (1)**   **VICTORIA GROUND**   23,327

Stoke City (1) 2 **Stein (32, 74)**	**Manchester United (0) 1** **Dublin (72)**

STOKE CITY: Prudhoe, Clarkson, Sandford, Cranson, Overson, Orlyggson, Gynn, Foley, Stein, Carruthers, Gleghorn.
SUBS: Kevin, Lowe, Muggleton.

MANCHESTER UNITED: Schmeichel, Martin, Irwin, Phelan, Kanchelskis, Pallister, Robson, Ferguson, McClair, Hughes, Dublin.
SUBS: Sharpe (for Robson), Bruce (for Phelan), Sealey.

The team that launched a thousand boos. The Stoke fans didn't like it when the boss decided to field this much-changed League Cup side, but I didn't hear many moans when Mark Stein hit two beauties. He not only gave them an advantage for the second leg but earned them a few quid when they sold him to Chelsea on the strength of this showing. It was our second upset in four games and we knew we had to do something to sort things out.

25 Sept.	FA CARLING PREMIERSHIP	OLD TRAFFORD	44,583

Manchester United (2) 4	Swindon Town (0) 2
Kanchelskis (4)	Mutch (78)
Cantona (40)	Bodin (87 pen)
Hughes (50, 80)	

MANCHESTER UNITED: Schmeichel, Parker, Irwin, Bruce, Sharpe, Pallister, Cantona, Ince, Keane, Hughes, Kanchelskis.
SUBS: McClair (for Sharpe), Giggs (for Kanchelskis), Sealey.

SWINDON TOWN: Digby, Summerbee, Bodin, Hazzard, Nijholt, Taylor, Moncur, Fjortoft, Ling, Mutch, Fenwick.
SUBS: White (for Fjortoft), MacLaren (for Moncur), Hammond.

Full marks to Swindon for trying to make a fight of it. They played some good football but we managed to stay on top after getting that early goal. Andrei Kanchelskis had a great game and showed the boss that he was worth a regular place in the side after being edged out for some of the opening games. His goal was a great solo run followed by a shot under Fraser Digby, our former reserve 'keeper.

P	W	D	L	F	A	PTS	PSN
9	7	1	1	19	6	22	1

29 Sept.	EUROPEAN CUP FIRST ROUND (2) OLD TRAFFORD	35,781

Manchester United (0) 2	Honved (0) 1
Bruce (55, 64)	Salloi (78)

MANCHESTER UNITED: Schmeichel, Parker, Irwin, Bruce, Sharpe, Pallister, Robson, Ince, Cantona, Hughes, Giggs.
SUBS: Phelan (for Ince), Martin (for Irwin), Dublin, Butt, Sealey.

HONVED: Brockhauser, Csabi, Plokai, Halmai, Banfi, Csehi, Illes, Szabados, Salloi, Vincze, Hamar.
SUBS: Orosz, Dragoner, Toth, Duro, Rott.

How many centre-halves play the last 26 minutes of a game looking for the goal to give them a hat trick? Steve Bruce got in two great headers, the first from an Irwin corner, the second from a Sharpe cross, and took us safely through to the second round of the Champions' Cup.

---

2 Oct.	FA CARLING PREMIERSHIP	HILLSBOROUGH	34,548

Sheffield Wednesday (0) 2	Manchester United (0) 3
Bart-Williams (47)	Hughes (50, 56)
Bright (86)	Giggs (71)

SHEFFIELD WEDNESDAY: Woods, Nilsson, Walker, Hyde, King, Palmer, Bart-Williams, Waddle, Sheridan, Bright, Sinton.
SUBS: Pearce, Jones, Pressman.

MANCHESTER UNITED: Schmeichel, Parker, Irwin, Bruce, Sharpe, Pallister, Cantona, Ince, Keane, Hughes, Giggs.
SUBS: McClair, Kanchelskis (for Giggs), Sealey.

Another cracking game for the Hillsborough fans. Perhaps not quite as dramatic as last season when we came back from 3–0 down to draw, but the Red Army enjoyed it. Sparky was in top form again and his two strikes swung the game our way. He and Eric Cantona combined to make the third which Ryan Giggs took well. Mark Bright pulled one back just before the end to make it an exciting finish.

P	W	D	L	F	A	PTS	PSN
10	8	1	1	22	8	25	1

6 Oct.   COCA-COLA CUP SECOND ROUND (2) OLD TRAFFORD   41, 387

Manchester United (0) 2	Stoke City (0) 0
Sharpe (46)	
McClair (88)	

MANCHESTER UNITED: Schmeichel, Martin, Irwin, Bruce, Sharpe, Pallister, Robson, Kanchelskis, McClair, Hughes, Keane.
SUBS: Giggs (for Martin), Ferguson, Sealey.

STOKE CITY: Muggleton, Clarkson, Cowans, Cranson, Overson, Orlyggson, Gynn, Foley, Stein, Sturridge, Gleghorn.
SUBS: Kevin, Carruthers (for Sturridge), Prudhoe.

Safely through to Round Three despite that scare in the first leg. Lee Sharpe scored his 5th of the season to level things just after half-time, and one or two people were thinking about an additional half an hour when Choccy hit the winner with his left foot. He has a remarkable record in the League Cup . . . thank goodness.

16 Oct.   FA CARLING PREMIERSHIP   OLD TRAFFORD   44,655

Manchester United (0) 2	Tottenham Hotspur (0) 1
Keane (66)	Caskey (72)
Sharpe (69)	

MANCHESTER UNITED: Schmeichel, Parker, Irwin, Bruce, Sharpe, Pallister, Cantona, Robson, Keane, Hughes, Giggs.
SUBS: McClair (for Robson), Butt (for Giggs), Sealey.

TOTTENHAM HOTSPUR: Thorstvedt, Kerslake, Campbell, Samways, Mabbutt, Sedgley, Dozzell, Caskey, Barmby, Sheringham, Howells.
SUBS: Moran (for Sheringham), Edinburgh (for Moran), Walker.

A comfortable win even though the scoreline makes it look a close game. Not very often do you see a substitute substituted but that's what happened to Paul Moran who came on in the first half and went off in the second. We scored twice within three minutes to lift things and look who was on the score sheet once again – sharp-shooting Sharpe!

P	W	D	L	F	A	PTS	PSN
11	9	1	1	24	9	28	1

---

20 Oct.   EUROPEAN CUP SECOND ROUND (1) OLD TRAFFORD   39,346

Manchester United (2) 3	Galatasaray (2) 3
Robson (3)	Erdem (16)
Hakan o. g. (13)	Kubilay (32, 63)
Cantona (81)	

MANCHESTER UNITED: Schmeichel, Martin, Sharpe, Bruce, Keane, Pallister, Robson, Ince, Cantona, Hughes, Giggs.
SUBS: Phelan (for Robson), Dublin, Butt, G. Neville, Sealey.

GALATASARAY: Hayrettin, Stumpf, Bulent, Ugur, Gotz, Tugay, Erdem, Hamza, Hakan, Suat, Kubilay.
SUBS: Mert, Yusuf (for Suat), Erdal (for Kubilay), Arsla, Nezihi.

Disaster. After leading 2–0 and looking to have the tie in our grasp, we let the Turks in when Arif Erdem scored an astonishing goal. Things went from bad to worse and before we knew it we were fighting to save our unbeaten home record in Europe. That record stayed intact thanks to Eric Cantona.

---

23 Oct.   FA CARLING PREMIERSHIP   GOODISON PARK   35,430

Everton (0) 0	Manchester United (0) 1
	Sharpe (53)

EVERTON: Southall, Holmes, Hinchcliffe, Watson, Ablett, Ward, Cottee, Horne, Beagrie, Ebbrell, Barlow.
SUBS: Preki (for Barlow), Jackson, Kearton.

MANCHESTER UNITED: Schmeichel, Martin, Irwin, Bruce, Sharpe, Pallister, Cantona, Ince, McClair, Hughes, Keane.
SUBS: Giggs, Phelan, Sealey.

Lee Sharpe's 7th goal of the season and it came at a crucial stage of the game. Everton went on to struggle to survive in the Premiership, but you would never have thought it on this showing. We have opened a 9-point gap at the top, with Norwich now second and Arsenal slipping to third.

P	W	D	L	F	A	PTS	PSN
12	10	1	1	25	9	31	1

---

27 Oct.	COCA-COLA CUP THIRD ROUND	OLD TRAFFORD	41,344

Manchester United (2) 5	Leicester City (0) 1
Bruce (7, 85)	Hill (65)
McClair (15)	
Sharpe (54)	
Hughes (62)	

MANCHESTER UNITED: Schmeichel, Phelan, Martin, Bruce, Sharpe, Pallister, Robson, Kanchelskis, McClair, Hughes, Keane.
SUBS: Irwin (for Pallister), Giggs (for Sharpe), Sealey.

LEICESTER CITY: Ward, Grayson, Lewis, Oldfield, Whitlow, Hill, Joachim, Thompson, Speedie, Agnew, Ormondroyd.
SUBS: Mills (for Lewis), Carey, Poole.

It was billed as the team most likely to win promotion against the reigning Premiership champions . . . and poor old Leicester never knew what hit them. They probably had second thoughts about trying to get into the First Division after this. It was one of those nights when everything went right . . . for us. That doesn't include Gary Pallister. He tried to do a Linford Christie, pulled a muscle and limped out of this game . . . and the next and the next.

30 Oct.	FA CARLING PREMIERSHIP	OLD TRAFFORD	44,663

Manchester United (0) 2 Cantona (53) Hughes (57)	**Queen's Park Rangers (1) 1** Allen (8)

MANCHESTER UNITED: Schmeichel, Parker, Irwin, Bruce, Sharpe, Phelan, Cantona, Ince, Keane, Hughes, Giggs.
SUBS: Martin, Kanchelskis, Sealey.

QPR: Stejskal, Bardsley, Peacock, McDonald, Wilson, Impey, Wilkins, Barker, Sinclair, Ferdinand, Allen.
SUBS: Yates, Holloway, Roberts.

My old mate Ray Wilkins seems to enjoy his trips back to Old Trafford and he was doing most of the smiling at half-time as we once again decided to let the opposition score first. Eric and Sparky hit back with 2 goals in 4 minutes and game 13 turned out lucky for us.

P	W	D	L	F	A	PTS	PSN
13	11	1	1	27	10	34	1

3 Nov.	EUROPEAN CUP SECOND ROUND (2) ISTANBUL	40,000

Galatasaray (0) 0 **Galatasaray won under the** **away goals rule**	**Manchester United (0) 0**

GALATASARAY: Hayrettin, Stumpf, Bulent, Yusuf, Gotz, Tugay, Erdem, Hamza, Hakan, Suat, Kubilay.
SUBS: Mert, Ugur, Erdal, Arsla, Nezihi.

MANCHESTER UNITED: Schmeichel, Parker, Irwin, Bruce, Sharpe, Phelan, Robson, Ince, Cantona, Keane, Giggs.
SUBS: Martin, Dublin (for Keane), Butt, G. Neville (for Phelan), Sealey.

No comment!

7 Nov.	FA CARLING PREMIERSHIP	MAINE ROAD	35,155

Manchester City (2) 2
Quinn (21, 32)

Manchester United (0) 3
Cantona (52, 78)
Keane (87)

MANCHESTER CITY: Coton, Edghill, Phelan, McMahon, Curle, Kernaghan, White, Sheron, Quinn, Flitcroft, Vonk.
SUBS: Lomas, Griffiths, Dibble

MANCHESTER UNITED: Schmeichel, Parker, Irwin, Bruce, Sharpe, Pallister, Cantona, Ince, Keane, Hughes, Kanchelskis.
SUBS: Giggs (for Kanchelskis), Robson, Sealey.

Heard the one about the two Irishmen and the Frenchman who combined to make a thrilling Manchester derby? Niall Quinn bagged two in the first half and we thought we had left our legs in Turkey as well as our hearts. Then Eric took over and hit two to level things and City were on the ropes when Roy Keane nipped in to score the winner.

P	W	D	L	F	A	PTS	PSN
14	12	1	1	30	12	37	1

20 Nov.	FA CARLING PREMIERSHIP	OLD TRAFFORD	44,748

Manchester United (0) 3
Pallister (54)
Hughes (64)
Kanchelskis (79)

Wimbledon (0) 1
Fashanu (62)

MANCHESTER UNITED: Schmeichel, Parker, Irwin, Bruce, Sharpe, Pallister, Cantona, Ince, Robson, Hughes, Kanchelskis.
SUBS: Giggs, Phelan (for Robson), Sealey.

WIMBLEDON: Segers, Barton, McAllister, Jones, Fitzgerald, Earle, Fashanu, Holdsworth, Scales, Joseph, Talboys.
SUBS: Clarke (for Holdsworth), Ardley, Digweed.

A good solid performance against the side which had beaten us at Old Trafford on their previous visit. The Dons did threaten when John Fashanu rubbed out Gary Pallister's only goal of the season but Mark and Andrei helped us to keep the gap between first and second at 11 points. We reckoned that we might need that cushion later in the season and we were right.

P	W	D	L	F	A	PTS	PSN
15	13	1	1	33	13	40	1

---

24 Nov.	FA CARLING PREMIERSHIP	OLD TRAFFORD	43,300

Manchester United (0) 0	**Ipswich Town (0) 0**

MANCHESTER UNITED: Schmeichel, Parker, Irwin, Bruce, Sharpe, Pallister, Cantona, Ince, Robson, Hughes, Kanchelskis.
SUBS: Giggs (for Kanchelskis), Ferguson (for Robson), Sealey.

IPSWICH TOWN: Forrest, Stockwell, Thompson, Mason, Wark, Linighan, Marshall, Kiwomya, Whelan, Youds, Palmer.
SUBS: Yallop (for Mason), Milton, Morgan.

A tactical victory for Ipswich? Perhaps. But with this kind of approach they could empty every ground in a couple of seasons. Negative attacking but solid defending meant a boring night out for most of the fans. Those who made the long journey from Suffolk can't possibly have enjoyed it. But Ipswich got what they came for and there was no denying them that.

P	W	D	L	F	A	PTS	PSN
16	13	2	1	33	13	41	1

27 Nov.	FA CARLING PREMIERSHIP	HIGHFIELD ROAD	17,020

Coventry (0) 0	Manchester United (0) 1
	Cantona (60)

COVENTRY: Ogrizovic, Atherton, Rennie, Babb, Morgan, Flynn, Boland, Darby, Ndlovu, Quinn, Wegerle.
SUBS: Williams (for Quinn), Marsden (for Boland), Gould.

MANCHESTER UNITED: Schmeichel, Parker, Irwin, Bruce, Sharpe, Pallister, Cantona, Ince, Ferguson, Hughes, Giggs.
SUBS: McClair, Robson, Sealey.

Same result as last season and another dour game. Coventry posed a threat at times but our defence stood firm and Eric Cantona picked up his 10th goal of the season with a neat close-range header after Ryan Giggs and Denis Irwin had combined in a run down the left. Big Peter had to pull off a couple of useful saves, but Steve Ogrizovic at the other end didn't exactly have an afternoon off.

P	W	D	L	F	A	PTS	PSN
17	14	2	1	34	13	44	1

30 Nov.	COCA-COLA CUP FOURTH ROUND	GOODISON PARK	34,052

Everton (0) 0	Manchester United (1) 2
	Hughes (13)
	Giggs (46)

EVERTON: Southall, Jackson, Hinchcliffe, Snodin, Watson, Ablett, Ward, Stuart, Cottee, Horne, Ebbrell.
SUBS: Preki (for Ward), Barlow (for Snodin), Kearton.

MANCHESTER UNITED: Schmeichel, Parker, Irwin, Bruce, Kanchelskis, Pallister, Cantona, Ince, Robson, Hughes, Giggs.
SUBS: McClair, Ferguson (for Robson), Sealey.

Here we are again. Less than six weeks after being at Goodison in the Premiership we had to face Everton in the League Cup with a similar outcome. Howard Kendall must have had nightmares about us in his final weeks in charge and Tony Cottee will be haunted by a penalty which would have put the Toffees back in the game if Peter Schmeichel had not saved it. Sparky's goal was a delight and it was quite a night for the Welsh as Giggsy popped in the second – but don't ask Nev Southall how he felt about it.

---

4 Dec.	FA CARLING PREMIERSHIP	OLD TRAFFORD	44,694

Manchester United (2) 2	**Norwich City (1) 2**
Giggs (30)	**Sutton (31)**
McClair (43)	**Fox (47 pen)**

MANCHESTER UNITED: Schmeichel, Parker, Irwin, Bruce, Kanchelskis, Pallister, Cantona, Ince, McClair, Hughes, Giggs.
SUBS: Sharpe (for Kanchelskis), Ferguson, Sealey.

NORWICH CITY: Gunn, Bowen, Newman, Culverhouse, Woodthorpe, Megson, Goss, Fox, Power, Butterworth, Sutton.
SUBS: Sutch (for Butterworth), Eadie (for Fox), Howie.

A good display by Norwich but for us it turned out to be two valuable home points dropped . . . again! We have discovered that it is getting easier to win away from Old Trafford because opponents are less likely to sit on a goal. Norwich had to chase us all the way and Chris Sutton gave a good display, showing everybody why he could be a summer transfer target.

P	W	D	L	F	A	PTS	PSN
18	14	3	1	36	15	45	1

| 7 Dec. | FA CARLING PREMIERSHIP | BRAMALL LANE | 26,746 |

Sheffield United (0) 0	Manchester United (2) 3
	Hughes (13)
	Sharpe (27)
	Cantona (60)

SHEFFIELD UNITED: Kelly, Gage, Nilsen, Beesley, Tuttle, Hoyland, Falconer, Ward, Bradshaw, Scott, Hodges.
SUBS: Flo (for Scott), Rogers (for Beesley), Muggleton.

MANCHESTER UNITED: Schmeichel, Parker, Irwin, Bruce, Sharpe, Pallister, Cantona, Ince, McClair, Hughes, Giggs.
SUBS: Kanchelskis, Keane (for McClair), Sealey.

One-way traffic and a comfortable win on a ground where things haven't exactly gone our way just lately. The Blades looked as though they needed a trip to the knife-sharpener and once again we showed that away from home we can be dangerous. Sheffield left the gaps and we were able to exploit them. It could have been many more than three.

P	W	D	L	F	A	PTS	PSN
19	15	3	1	39	15	48	1

| 11 Dec. | FA CARLING PREMIERSHIP | ST JAMES'S PARK | 36,388 |

| Newcastle United (0) 1 | Manchester United (0) 1 |
| Cole (71) | Ince (60) |

NEWCASTLE UNITED: Hooper, Watson, Venison, Howey, Elliott, Lee, Bracewell, Clarke, Sellars, Cole, Beardsley.
SUBS: O'Brien, Srnicek, Allen.

MANCHESTER UNITED: Schmeichel, Parker, Irwin, Bruce, Sharpe, Pallister, Cantona, Ince, McClair, Hughes, Giggs.
SUBS: Kanchelskis (for Hughes), Keane (for McClair), Sealey.

This one was billed as the day we would get our come-uppance but Incey scored first and Newcastle had to fight all the way to earn themselves a home point. It was a cracking game and the fans had value for money. Our first away draw of the season in the Premiership, and that man Cole scored again. They always say: 'Where would Newcastle be without its Cole?' Now we know what that means!

P	W	D	L	F	A	PTS	PSN
20	15	4	1	40	16	49	1

---

19 Dec.	FA CARLING PREMIERSHIP	OLD TRAFFORD	44,499

Manchester United (1) 3	**Aston Villa (0) 1**
Cantona (21, 88)	**Cox (90)**
Ince (89)	

MANCHESTER UNITED: Schmeichel, Parker, Irwin, Bruce, Sharpe, Pallister, Cantona, Ince, Keane, Hughes, Kanchelskis.
SUBS: Giggs (for Sharpe), McClair, Sealey.

ASTON VILLA: Bosnich, Barrett, Cox, Teale, McGrath, Richardson, Small, Parker, Saunders, Atkinson, Whittingham.
SUBS: Daley (for Saunders), Cowans, Spink.

Not what we have come to expect from games against Villa. Their challenge for the League seemed to have faded as we reached the halfway stage. They started this game in 8th place and finished 9th, 21 points adrift. But their day would come later in the season as we discovered. Eric's brace took his tally to 13 goals – unlucky for some, but not us.

P	W	D	L	F	A	PTS	PSN
21	16	4	1	43	17	52	1

26 Dec.	FA CARLING PREMIERSHIP	OLD TRAFFORD	44,511

Manchester United (0) 1 **Ince (88)**	**Blackburn Rovers (1) 1** **Gallacher (16)**

MANCHESTER UNITED: Schmeichel, Parker, Irwin, Bruce, Sharpe, Pallister, Cantona, Ince, Keane, Hughes, Giggs.
SUBS: McClair (for Parker), Ferguson (for Hughes), Sealey.

BLACKBURN ROVERS: Flowers, Berg, May, Hendry, Le Saux, Ripley, Sherwood, Batty, Shearer, Newell, Gallacher.
SUBS: Wilcox (for Gallacher), Marker, Mimms.

Almost a smash and grab raid by Kenny and his boys. Rovers got the goal they hoped for early in the game and then defended in numbers as we hurled everything at them. In the end it took a late goal from Incey to save our blushes, but Blackburn had thrown down the gauntlet and we knew they would give us a good chase for the championship. They were 14 points adrift with a game in hand at this stage.

P	W	D	L	F	A	PTS	PSN
22	16	5	1	44	18	53	1

29 Dec.	FA CARLING PREMIERSHIP	BOUNDARY PARK	16,708

Oldham Athletic (2) 2 **Sharp (15)** **Holden (25)**	**Manchester United (3) 5** **Kanchelskis (4)** **Cantona (19 pen)** **Bruce (39)** **Giggs (53, 59)**

OLDHAM ATHLETIC: Hallworth, Fleming, Pedersen, Jobson, Makin, Halle, Milligan, Bernard, Graham, Sharp, Holden.
SUBS: Adams (for Graham), Ritchie, Gerrard.

MANCHESTER UNITED: Schmeichel, Parker, Irwin, Bruce, Sharpe,

Pallister, Cantona, Ince, Keane, Kanchelskis, Giggs.
SUBS: McClair (for Cantona), Robson (for Ince), Sealey.

Typical of the clashes with Latics, who are like one of those pop-up toys – everytime you think you have got them on the floor they spring back again. Andrei was outstanding in this game and Ryan scored two important goals.

P	W	D	L	F	A	PTS	PSN
23	17	5	1	49	20	56	1

1 Jan.	FA CARLING PREMIERSHIP	OLD TRAFFORD	44,724

Manchester United (0) 0	**Leeds United (0) 0**

MANCHESTER UNITED: Schmeichel, Parker, Irwin, Bruce, Robson, Pallister, Cantona, Keane, McClair, Kanchelskis, Giggs.
SUBS: Dublin, Ferguson, Sealey.

LEEDS UNITED: Beeney, Kelly, Dorigo, White, Fairclough, Newsome, Strachan, Pemberton, Deane, McAllister, Hodge.
SUBS: Wetherall, Sharp (for Hodge), Lukic.

If the Oldham game was typical then so too was this one. A dour struggle against a Leeds side which fancied its chances in the championship stakes. But you have to win games to win titles, especially away from home, and while we were disappointed that it was our fifth home draw we stayed firmly on top.

P	W	D	L	F	A	PTS	PSN
24	17	6	1	49	20	57	1

4 Jan.	FA CARLING PREMIERSHIP ANFIELD	42,795

Liverpool (2) 3 Clough (24, 37) Ruddock (79)	**Manchester United (3) 3** Bruce (9) Giggs (20) Irwin (23)

LIVERPOOL: Grobbelaar, Jones, Dicks, Wright, Clough, Rush, Barnes, Redknapp, McManaman, Fowler, Ruddock.
SUBS: Nicol, Bjornebye (for Clough), James.

MANCHESTER UNITED: Schmeichel, Parker, Irwin, Bruce, Keane, Pallister, Cantona, Ince, McClair, Kanchelskis, Giggs.
SUBS: Robson, Ferguson, Sealey.

The boss was not amused as we threw away a 3-goal lead and at Anfield of all places. Yet we could easily have been trailing before Brucie got our first. It was a tremendous advert for football and everybody who was there must have enjoyed it even if their side didn't win.

P	W	D	L	F	A	PTS	PSN
25	17	7	1	52	23	58	1

9 Jan.	FA CUP ROUND THREE BRAMALL LANE	22,019

Sheffield United (0) 0	**Manchester United (0) 1** Hughes (62)

SHEFFIELD UNITED: Kelly, Bradshaw, Gage, Tuttle, Beesley, Hoyland, Ward, Kamara, Flo, Hodges, Whitehouse.
SUBS: Scott (for Hoyland), Nilsen (for Ward), Muggleton.

MANCHESTER UNITED: Schmeichel, Parker, Irwin, Bruce, Kanchelskis, Pallister, Cantona, Ince, Keane, Hughes, Giggs.
SUBS: McClair, Robson, Sealey.

Three games against The Blades and 3 wins, this one setting us off on the road towards the double. Last season Sheffield had knocked us out of the Cup on their way to the semi-final. We fancied going a bit further.

12 Jan.	COCA-COLA CUP FIFTH ROUND	OLD TRAFFORD	43,794

Manchester United (1) 2 Giggs (28) Cantona (60)	Portsmouth (1) 2 Walsh (32, 70)

MANCHESTER UNITED: Schmeichel, Parker, Irwin, Bruce, Kanchelskis, Pallister, Cantona, Robson, McClair, Hughes, Giggs.
SUBS: Keane (for Hughes), Dublin (for McClair), Sealey.

PORTSMOUTH: Knight, Durnin, Daniel, McLoughlin, Symons, Awford, Stimson, Dobson, Powell, Walsh, Kristensen.
SUBS: Chamberlain (for Symons), Doling (for Stimson), Horne.

Paul Walsh scored twice to keep Pompey's hopes alive and he couldn't have chosen a better time to put on such a good performance, because he was was being watched by Manchester City – and they bought him later in the season. Has our Coca-Cola Cup campaign lost its fizz? We'll find out in a fortnight.

15 Jan.	FA CARLING PREMIERSHIP	WHITE HART LANE	31,343

Tottenham Hotspur (0) 0	Manchester United (0) 1 Hughes (49)

TOTTENHAM HOTSPUR: Walker, Edinburgh, Samways, Calderwood, Barmby, Anderton, Sedgley, Hazard, Caskey, Kerslake, Campbell.
SUBS: Austin (for Edinburgh), Hendry, Day.

MANCHESTER UNITED: Schmeichel, Parker, Irwin, Bruce, Kanchelskis, Pallister, Cantona, Ince, Keane, Hughes, Giggs.
SUBS: McClair (for Hughes), Dublin, Sealey.

After drawing three out of the last four Premiership games this got us back on the road again and we never felt in any danger from Spurs. Things were starting to happen behind us though. Blackburn were still 13 points adrift, but they had hit a winning streak and had 2 games in hand.

P	W	D	L	F	A	PTS	PSN
26	18	7	1	53	23	61	1

---

22 Jan.	FA CARLING PREMIERSHIP	OLD TRAFFORD	44,750

Manchester United (1) 1	**Everton (0) 0**
Giggs (26)	

MANCHESTER UNITED: Schmeichel, Parker, Irwin, Bruce, Kanchelskis, Pallister, Cantona, Ince, Keane, Hughes, Giggs.
SUBS: McClair, Dublin, Sealey.

EVERTON: Southall, Jackson, Moore, Snodin, Ebrell, Ablett, Stuart, Angell, Cottee, Warzycha, Beagrie.
SUBS: Hinchcliffe (for Warzycha), Barlow (for Cottee), Kearton.

Mike Walker's first visit to Old Trafford as manager of Everton and one which he will remember not so much for the result but for the occasion. This was the first game following Sir Matt's death and the Everton supporters rightfully earned our praise for their impeccable behaviour. As for the game, it was a fitting performance by the lads who played some amazing football against an Everton side which really made a contest of it.

P	W	D	L	F	A	PTS	PSN
27	19	7	1	54	23	64	1

---

26 Jan.   COCA-COLA CUP FIFTH ROUND (R)   FRATTON PARK   24,950

| Portsmouth (0) 0 | Manchester United (1) 1 |
| | McClair (27) |

PORTSMOUTH: Knight, Durnin, Daniel, McLoughlin, Symons, Awford, Neil, Chamberlain, Creaney, Walsh, Kristensen.
SUBS: Powell (for Chamberlain), Dobson, Horne.

MANCHESTER UNITED: Schmeichel, Parker, Irwin, Bruce, Kanchelskis, Pallister, Cantona, Ince, McClair, Keane, Giggs.
SUBS: Dublin, G. Neville, Sealey.

After their great performance at Old Trafford the home fans must have expected big things from Pompey, but we totally controlled the game and even though there was only one goal it was an easy win. Another Choccy strike to put us through to the semi-finals . . . he must have a garage full of Coca-Cola!

---

30 Jan.   FA CUP ROUND FOUR   CARROW ROAD   21,060

Norwich City (0) 0	Manchester United (1) 2
	Keane (19)
	Cantona (73)

NORWICH CITY: Gunn, Culverhouse, Newman, Polston, Woodthorpe, Goss, Megson, Crook, Bowen, Sutton, Fox.
SUBS: Ekoku (for Crook), Butterworth, Howie.

MANCHESTER UNITED: Schmeichel, Parker, Irwin, Bruce, Kanchelskis, Pallister, Cantona, Ince, Keane, Hughes, Giggs.
SUBS: McClair (for Hughes), Dublin, Sealey.

Passions were high for this Sunday FA Cup clash and it was a battle all the way as we realized that if we were going to get to Wembley it would be by the long route. In the end a comfortable win thanks to goals from Keano and Eric, but we really came under the television microscope.

| 5 Feb. | FA CARLING PREMIERSHIP | LOFTUS ROAD | 21,267 |

Queen's Park Rangers (1) 2	Manchester United (2) 3
Wilson (44 pen)	Kanchelskis (18)
Ferdinand (64)	Cantona (45)
	Giggs (59)

QPR: Stejskal, Bardsley, Wilson, Wilkins, Peacock, Yates, Barker, Holloway, Ferdinand, Penrice, Sinclair.
SUBS: Meaker (for Sinclair), Brevett, Roberts.

MANCHESTER UNITED: Schmeichel, Parker, Irwin, Bruce, Kanchelskis, Pallister, Cantona, Ince, Keane, Hughes, Giggs.
SUBS: McClair, Dublin, Sealey.

Quite a game this one for the neutral spectator and once more 3 valuable points away from home. Those experts who thought the race would be over by now are having second thoughts but we are still on course for retaining that championship. The lead remains 13 points, but Rovers have 2 games in hand so hope to cut it to 7 . . . But I'd settle for that.

P	W	D	L	F	A	PTS	PSN
28	20	7	1	57	25	67	1

| 13 Feb. | COCA-COLA CUP SEMI-FINAL(1) | OLD TRAFFORD | 43,294 |

Manchester United (1) 1	Sheffield Wednesday (0) 0
Giggs (19)	

MANCHESTER UNITED: Schmeichel, Parker, Irwin, Bruce, Kanchelskis, Pallister, Cantona, Ince, Keane, Hughes, Giggs.
SUBS: McClair, Dublin, Sealey.

SHEFFIELD WEDNESDAY: Pressman, Nilsson, Pearce, Walker, Coleman, Waddle, Hyde, Palmer, Sinton, Hirst, Bright.
SUBS: Bart-Williams (for Waddle), Watson, Woods.

One game away from Wembley and a 1-goal lead to take to Hillsborough. Will it be enough? On our away form we fancy our chances against anybody, but Wednesday made it tough for us in front of our own fans by trying to stop us from scoring. Thankfully Giggsy was on the ball, intercepting a Nilsson back-pass and scoring a lovely solo goal.

---

20 Feb.	FA CUP ROUND FIVE	SELHURST PARK	27,511

Wimbledon (0) 0	Manchester United (1) 3
	Cantona (39)
	Ince (63)
	Irwin (71)

WIMBLEDON: Segers, Barton, Jones, Fitzgerald, Earle, Fashanu, Holdsworth, Scales, Fear, Elkins, Blissett.
SUBS: Blackwell, Sullivan, Clarke.

MANCHESTER UNITED: Schmeichel, Parker, Irwin, Bruce, Kanchelskis, Pallister, Cantona, Ince, Keane, Hughes, Giggs.
SUBS: McClair (for Cantona), Dublin (for Hughes), Sealey.

Another cup-tie away from home and we were told we were in for a bit of a pasting this particular afternoon. But we had other ideas. Wimbledon were given a run-around and we could have had more goals, but 3 was enough to take us through to the quarter-finals . . . and guess what, we got a home draw!

| 26 Feb. | FA CARLING PREMIERSHIP | UPTON PARK | 28,832 |

West Ham United (0) 2	Manchester United (1) 2
Chapman (69)	Hughes (6)
Morley (73)	Ince (87)

WEST HAM UNITED: Miklosko, Breacker, Martin, Potts, Burrows, Marsh, M. Allen, Bishop, Holmes, Morley, Chapman.
SUBS: C. Allen, Rowland, Kelly.

MANCHESTER UNITED: Schmeichel, Parker, Irwin, Bruce, Kanchelskis, Pallister, Cantona, Ince, McClair, Hughes, Keane.
SUBS: Dublin (for Kanchelskis), Thornley (for Irwin), Sealey.

There was double delight in the camp when Incey scored a late equalizer against his old club. Firstly it saved us from defeat after we had led early on, and secondly it shoved the racist taunts he had been subjected to back down the throats of the fans who once cheered him. Ben Thornley got on for a taste of the big time.

P	W	D	L	F	A	PTS	PSN
29	20	8	1	59	27	68	1

| 2 Mar. | COCA-COLA CUP SEMI-FINAL (2) | HILLSBOROUGH | 34,878 |

Sheffield Wednesday (1) 1	Manchester United (3) 4
Hyde (33)	McClair (4)
	Kanchelskis (11)
	Hughes (38, 82)

SHEFFIELD WEDNESDAY: Pressman, Nilsson, Pearce, Walker, Coleman, Bart-Williams, Hyde, Palmer, Sinton, Hirst, Bright.
SUBS: Watson (for Sinton), Poric, Key.

MANCHESTER UNITED: Schmeichel, Parker, Irwin, Bruce, Kanchelskis, Pallister, Keane, Ince, McClair, Hughes, Giggs.
SUBS: Robson, Dublin, Sealey

I'm not the best of spectators when I'm on the bench but I would have paid to watch this display. We booked our ticket to Wembley by taking the game to Wednesday from the first minute and they had no answer. Do I need to point out that Brian McClair yet again scored a cup goal? That was his 4th in this competition.

---

5 Mar.	FA CARLING PREMIERSHIP	OLD TRAFFORD	44,745

Manchester United (0) 0	**Chelsea (0) 1** **Peacock (64)**

MANCHESTER UNITED: Schmeichel, Parker, Irwin, Bruce, Kanchelskis, Pallister, Keane, Ince, McClair, Hughes, Giggs.
SUBS: Robson (for McClair), Dublin (for Parker), Sealey.

CHELSEA: Kharine, Clarke, Kjeldbjerg, Johnsen, Sinclair, Burley, Newton, Peacock, Wise, Stein, Spencer.
SUBS: Hoddle, Hopkin (for Stein), Hitchcock.

Now this really put the cat amongst the Peacocks. Gavin did it again just as he did at Stamford Bridge, but in truth we murdered Chelsea 0–1! Boarding up the goalmouth seemed to work for Kharine who was in superb form. We had an inquest in the dressing-room about who had walked under a ladder on the way to Old Trafford . . . it turned out to be all of us!

P	W	D	L	F	A	PTS	PSN
30	20	8	2	59	28	68	1

---

12 Mar.	FA CUP ROUND SIX	OLD TRAFFORD	44,347

Manchester United (0) 3 **Hughes (46)** **Kanchelskis (72, 76)**	**Charlton Athletic (0) 1** **Leaburn (77)**

MANCHESTER UNITED: Schmeichel, Parker, Irwin, Bruce, Kanchelskis, Pallister, Cantona, Ince, Keane, Hughes, Giggs.

SUBS: McClair, Robson, Sealey (for Parker).

CHARLTON ATHLETIC: Vaughan, Brown, McCleary, Balmer, Minto, M. Robson, Pitcher, Pardew, Nelson, Grant, Leaburn.
SUBS: Walsh (for Grant), Chapple, Bolder.

Peter Schmeichel was sent off just before half-time and the gaffer had to do a bit of juggling. He pulled Paul Parker out of the game as Les Sealey took over in goal and we played with 10 men for the whole of the second half. It seemed to do the trick because we ran Charlton ragged to book our place in the semi-final.

16 Mar.	FA CARLING PREMIERSHIP	OLD TRAFFORD	43,669

Manchester United (4) 5	Sheffield Wednesday (0) 0
Giggs (14)	
Hughes (15)	
Ince (21)	
Cantona (44, 55)	

MANCHESTER UNITED: Schmeichel, Parker, Irwin, Bruce, Kanchelskis, Pallister, Cantona, Ince, Keane, Hughes, Giggs.
SUBS: McClair (for Giggs), Robson (for Kanchelskis), Sealey.

SHEFFIELD WEDNESDAY: Pressman, Nilsson, Pearce, Walker, Coleman, King, Bart-Williams, Poric, Watts, Sinton, Bright.
SUBS: Watson (for Nilsson), Jemson, Woods.

If Trevor Francis had come into our dressing-room at half-time waving a white flag nobody would have been surprised. This was Manchester United at their best and no team would have lived with us. Blackburn were closing in so it was time for action and we did our stuff.

P	W	D	L	F	A	PTS	PSN
31	21	8	2	64	28	71	1

| 19 Mar. | FA CARLING PREMIERSHIP | COUNTY GROUND | 18,102 |

Swindon Town (1) 2	Manchester United (1) 2
Nijholt (35)	Keane (13)
Fjortoft (82)	Ince (62)

SWINDON TOWN: Digby, Whitbread, Kilcline, Taylor, Horlock, Sanchez, Summerbee, Moncur, Nijholt, McAvennie, Fjortoft.
SUBS: Ling (for Horlock), Scott (for McAvennie), Hammond.

MANCHESTER UNITED: Schmeichel, Parker, Irwin, Bruce, Keane, Pallister, Cantona, Ince, McClair, Hughes, Giggs.
SUBS: Dublin, Phelan, Sealey.

Eric Cantona's nightmare begins when he is sent off for stamping on John Moncur after the two of them had tangled on the ground. This was a game of top against bottom and Swindon wanted to show their fans that they had some fight left. They did well to hold us and deserved their point.

P	W	D	L	F	A	PTS	PSN
32	21	9	2	66	30	72	1

| 22 Mar. | FA CARLING PREMIERSHIP | HIGHBURY | 36,203 |

Arsenal (1) 2	Manchester United (1) 2
Pallister o.g. (37)	Sharpe (10, 53)
Merson (77)	

ARSENAL: Seaman, Dixon, Winterburn, Davis, Bould, Adams, Jensen, Wright, Smith, Merson, Selley.
SUBS: Keown, Campbell (for Davis), Miller.

MANCHESTER UNITED: Schmeichel, Parker, Irwin, Bruce, Sharpe, Pallister, Cantona, Ince, Keane, Hughes, Giggs.
SUBS: McClair (for Sharpe), Robson, Sealey.

Another red card for Eric! Yes, the Frenchman is sent off again, this time for two bookable offences, but television evidence later proved that he was harshly treated. Referee Vic Callow is off Eric's Christmas card list, and now we can feel the hot breath of Blackburn Rovers down our necks.

P	W	D	L	F	A	PTS	PSN
33	21	10	2	68	32	73	1

---

27 Mar.	COCA-COLA CUP FINAL	WEMBLEY STATIUM	77,231

Aston Villa (1) 3	Manchester United (0) 1
Atkinson (25)	Hughes (83)
Saunders (76, 89 pen)	

ASTON VILLA: Bosnich, Barrett, Staunton, Teale, McGrath, Richardson, Saunders, Daley, Townsend, Atkinson, Fenton.
SUBS: Cox (for Staunton), Houghton, Spink.

MANCHESTER UNITED: Sealey, Parker, Irwin, Bruce, Kanchelskis, Pallister, Cantona, Ince, Keane, Hughes, Giggs.
SUBS: Sharpe (for Giggs), McClair (for Bruce), Walsh.

Unbelievably another player is sent off, our fourth in five games. This time it's Andrei Kanchelskis who is judged to have deliberately handled the ball in the last minute. The game was more or less over and it was a sad ending to a poor performance. Villa tied up midfield and we never really got into gear. At least this ended all the paper talk about the treble . . . but the double was still in sight.

| 30 Mar. | FA CARLING PREMIERSHIP | OLD TRAFFORD | 44,751 |

Manchester United (1) 1
Ince (37)

Liverpool (0) 0

MANCHESTER UNITED: Schmeichel, Parker, Irwin, Bruce, Sharpe, Pallister, Cantona, Ince, Keane, Hughes, Kanchelskis.
SUBS: Giggs (for Sharpe), Robson (for Cantona), Sealey.

LIVERPOOL: James, Jones, Dicks, Ruddock, Nicol, McManaman, Redknapp, Whelan, Rush, Barnes, Thomas.
SUBS: Fowler (for Thomas), Clough, Grobbelaar.

A first visit to Old Trafford in his role as Liverpool manager for Roy Evans, a former member of their backroom staff, and he was none too pleased about a penalty decision which his side was refused. Television proved that Keith Hackett was wrong – then right. He wrongly gave Liverpool a spot kick, then changed his mind when his linesman told him that he'd made a mistake. Coming up next, Blackburn.

P	W	D	L	F	A	PTS	PSN
34	22	10	2	69	32	76	1

| 2 Apr. | FA CARLING PREMIERSHIP | EWOOD PARK | 20,886 |

Blackburn Rovers (0) 2
Shearer (46, 76)

Manchester United (0) 0

BLACKBURN ROVERS: Flowers, May, Sherwood, Hendry, Le Saux, Ripley, Shearer, Newell, Wilcox, Berg, Batty.
SUBS: Marker (for Newell), Wright, Mimms.

MANCHESTER UNITED: Schmeichel, Parker, Irwin, Bruce, Sharpe, Pallister, Kanchelskis, Ince, Keane, Hughes, Giggs.
SUBS: McClair (for Parker), Robson, Sealey.

Blackburn were fired up for this one and deserved their win. Alan Shearer bagged two great goals and they made their intentions clear from the start. Their supporters were convinced that the championship was in the bag, but I can assure you that we had very different ideas. Our lead is just 3 points.

P	W	D	L	F	A	PTS	PSN
35	22	10	3	69	34	76	1

4 Apr.	FA CARLING PREMIERSHIP	OLD TRAFFORD	44,686

Manchester United (1) 3	**Oldham Athletic (0) 2**
Giggs (17)	**McCarthy (50)**
Dublin (66)	**Sharp (70)**
Ince (67)	

MANCHESTER UNITED: Schmeichel, Keane, Irwin, Bruce, Sharpe, Pallister, Kanchelskis, Ince, McClair, Hughes, Giggs.
SUBS: Robson, Dublin (for McClair), Sealey.

OLDHAM ATHLETIC: Hallworth, Makin, Jobson, Redmond, Pointon, Fleming, Milligan, Brennan, Holden, McCarthy, Sharp.
SUBS: Beckford (for Makin), Palmer (for Brennan), Gerrard.

The first of three clashes with Latics and one which typified their fighting spirit. We looked to have the game tied up, but they came back at us and made us hang on to the end. We needed these 3 points as much as they did, but unfortunately they couldn't get enough from their remaining games to stay up.

P	W	D	L	F	A	PTS	PSN
36	23	10	3	72	36	79	1

| 10 Apr. | FA CUP SEMI-FINAL | WEMBLEY STADIUM | 56,399 |

| Oldham Athletic (0) 1 | Manchester United (0) 1 [a. e. t.] |
| Pointon (106) | Hughes (119) |

OLDHAM ATHLETIC: Hallworth, Makin, Jobson, Fleming, Pointon, Bernard, Milligan, Henry, Holden, Beckford, Sharp.
SUBS: Brennan, Ritchie, Gerrard.

MANCHESTER UNITED: Schmeichel, Parker, Irwin, Bruce, Sharpe, Pallister, Dublin, Ince, McClair, Hughes, Giggs.
SUBS: Robson (for Dublin), Butt (for Parker), Sealey.

We played 120 minutes but as far as we were concerned 119 didn't matter. Sparky scored a vital goal with only seconds of extra time remaining, and no-one will know what might have happened had he missed the target. Latics were ready for the final . . . but we had other ideas.

| 13 Apr. | FA CUP SEMI-FINAL (R) | MAINE ROAD | 32,311 |

Manchester United (2) 4	Oldham Athletic (1) 1
Irwin (10)	Pointon (40)
Kanchelskis (15)	
Robson (62)	
Giggs (67)	

MANCHESTER UNITED: Schmeichel, Parker, Irwin, Bruce, Kanchelskis, Pallister, Robson, Ince, Keane, Hughes, Giggs.
SUBS: Sharpe (for Hughes), McClair (for Keane), Sealey.

OLDHAM ATHLETIC: Hallworth, Makin, Jobson, Fleming, Pointon, Bernard, Milligan, Henry, Holden, Beckford, Sharp.
SUBS: Redmond (for Pointon), Ritchie (for Beckford), Gerrard.

My last goal for United and my 99th since joining the club. I suppose it turned out to be a pretty important one. It came as

Latics were trying to fight back, but we had the game under control and found ourselves at Wembley for the 4th time in a season, with Chelsea as opponents – the only side to have beaten us twice! Script by Agatha Christie?

---

16 Apr.	FA CARLING PREMIERSHIP SELHURST PARK	28,553

Wimbledon (1) 1 **Fashanu (21)**	**Manchester United (0) 0**

WIMBLEDON: Segers, Barton, Jones, Blackwell, Earle, Fashanu, Holdsworth, Scales, Gayle, Fear, Elkins.
SUBS: Perry, Sullivan, Blissett.

MANCHESTER UNITED: Schmeichel, Parker, Irwin, Bruce, Kanchelskis, Pallister, Robson, Ince, McClair, Hughes, Giggs.
SUBS: Sharpe (for Robson), Dublin (for Parker), Sealey.

Tension mounts at the top and both runners stumble as they take a difficult fence. We go down to the Dons with an indifferent performance after Blackburn have been beaten 3–1 by struggling Southampton. Goal difference separates the sides at the moment, but we have a game in hand. So for the final run-in.

P	W	D	L	F	A	PTS	PSN
37	23	10	4	72	37	79	1

---

23 Apr.	FA CARLING PREMIERSHIP OLD TRAFFORD	44,333

Manchester United (2) 2 **Cantona (39, 44)**	**Manchester City (0) 0**

MANCHESTER UNITED: Schmeichel, Parker, Irwin, Bruce, Sharpe, Pallister, Cantona, Ince, Keane, Hughes, Kanchelskis.
SUBS: Giggs (for Sharpe), Robson, Walsh

MANCHESTER CITY: Dibble, Hill, Curle, Vonk, D. Brightwell, Karl, McMahon, Rocastle, Beagrie, Walsh, Rossler.
SUBS: I. Brightwell (for Karl), Lomas, Margetson.

Eric's back! Monsieur Cantona returns from his 5-match suspension which followed those two sendings-off, and boy does he return. Two goals in the space of 5 minutes destroy City's hopes. They had come to Old Trafford confident that they could dent our championship hopes but there was no chance of that happening. With 4 games to go we head the table by 4 points.

P	W	D	L	F	A	PTS	PSN
38	24	10	4	74	37	82	1

---

27 Apr.	FA CARLING PREMIERSHIP ELLAND ROAD	41,125

Leeds United (0) 0	Manchester United (0) 2
	Kanchelskis (48)
	Giggs (84)

LEEDS UNITED: Lukic, Kelly, Newsome, Wetherall, Dorigo, Strachan, Fairclough, McAllister, Speed, Wallace, Deane.
SUBS: Pemberton (for Dorigo), Whelan (for Wetherall), Beeney.

MANCHESTER UNITED: Schmeichel, Parker, Irwin, Bruce, Kanchelskis, Pallister, Cantona, Ince, Keane, Hughes, Giggs.
SUBS: McClair, Robson, Walsh.

Many people say that this was the night when we retained the championship. If we had lost we could have had a struggle in the closing games. This was a comfortable victory with Andrei and Ryan topping good performances with their goals. Three games to go and we have to be cautious because Blackburn could still overtake us if we slip.

P	W	D	L	F	A	PTS	PSN
39	25	10	4	76	37	85	1

| 1 May | FA CARLING PREMIERSHIP | PORTMAN ROAD | 22,559 |

| **Ipswich Town (1) 1**
Kiwomya (19) | **Manchester United (1) 2**
Cantona (35)
Giggs (47) |

IPSWICH TOWN: Forrest, Stockwell, Linighan, Johnson, Whelan, Wark, Palmer, Williams, Milton, Marshall, Kiwomya.
SUBS: Youds (for Johnson), Guentchev (for Whelan), Baker.

MANCHESTER UNITED: Schmeichel, Parker, Irwin, Bruce, Kanchelskis, Pallister, Cantona, Ince, Keane, Hughes, Giggs.
SUBS: Sharpe (for Giggs), McClair, Walsh (for Schmeichel).

Drama in the last stages of the season. We're top and heading for the title but Peter Schmeichel is doubtful for the FA Cup Final after damaging ankle ligaments as he tried a clearance on the edge of his penalty area. Gary Walsh takes over and will play in the last two Premiership games . . . and who knows perhaps even the final itself.

P	W	D	L	F	A	PTS	PSN
40	26	10	4	78	38	88	1

| 4 May | FA CARLING PREMIERSHIP | OLD TRAFFORD | 44,705 |

| **Manchester United (0) 2**
Kanchelskis (60)
Hughes (89) | **Southampton (0) 0** |

SOUTHAMPTON: Beasant, Kenna, Monkou, Widdrington, Benali, Charlton, Allen, Magilton, Maddison, Le Tissier, Dowie.
SUBS: Maskell (for Widdrington), Dodd, Andrews.

MANCHESTER UNITED: Walsh, Parker, Irwin, Kanchelskis, Sharpe, Pallister, Cantona, Ince, Keane, Hughes, Giggs.
SUBS: McClair, Robson, Sealey.

Champions again! Yes, we've done it. Blackburn slipped at Coventry and ended their chase and even without this win over Alan Ball's struggling side we had taken the title. I announced my intentions of leaving Old Trafford at the end of the season, and that my last home game would be against Coventry on the day the Premiership Trophy would be handed back to us. What a way to go!

P	W	D	L	F	A	PTS	PSN
41	27	10	4	80	38	91	1

---

8 May	FA CARLING PREMIERSHIP	OLD TRAFFORD	44,717

Manchester United (0) 0	Coventry City (0) 0

MANCHESTER UNITED: Walsh, G. Neville, Irwin, Bruce, Sharpe, Pallister, Cantona, Robson, McClair, McKee, Dublin.
SUBS: Parker (for Bruce), Keane (for McKee), Sealey.

COVENTRY CITY: Ogrizovic, Borrows, Morgan, Atherton, Babb, Rennie, Boland, Darby, Jenkinson, Flynn, Ndlovu.
SUBS: Pickering, Quinn, Gould.

The end of my 13 years at United and an afternoon of mixed feelings. I was delighted that we had retained the championship but I was sad to be leaving so many friends. I would dearly have loved to have got my 100th goal for the club, but my one chance went inches wide of the post. The Premiership Trophy won, there was one more target before the season closed.

P	W	D	L	F	A	PTS	PSN
42	27	11	4	80	38	92	1

14 May	FA CUP FINAL	WEMBLEY STADIUM	79,634

Manchester United (0) 4
Cantona (61 pen, 66 pen)
Hughes (68)
McClair (89)

Chelsea (0) 0

MANCHESTER UNITED: Schmeichel, Parker, Irwin, Bruce, Kanchelskis, Pallister, Cantona, Ince, Keane, Hughes, Giggs.
SUBS: Sharpe (for Kanchelskis), McClair (for Irwin), Walsh.

CHELSEA: Kharine, Clarke, Kjeldberg, Johnsen, Sinclair, Burley, Newton, Peacock, Wise, Stein, Spencer.
SUBS: Hoddle (for Burley), Cascarino (for Stein), Hitchcock.

Manchester United become the fourth club this century to win the League and Cup double. It was a great honour for me to be a part of it. I would have loved to have been involved in the Final, but the manager had to look to the future and used the players who would still be with him next season. I only wish I was 10 years younger!

APPEARANCES

	LGE	FA	LC	EC	CS	SUB
Schmeichel	40	7	8	4	1	–
Parker	39	7	6	3	1	1
Irwin	42	7	8	3	1	1
Bruce	41	7	8	4	1	1
Kanchelskis	28	6	9	–	1	3
Pallister	41	7	9	3	1	–
Cantona	34	5	5	4	1	–
Ince	39	7	5	4	1	–
Keane	34	6	6	3	1	4
Hughes	36	7	8	2	1	–
Giggs	32	7	6	4	1	8
Sharpe	26	1	2	4	–	9
McClair	12	1	6	–	–	18
Robson	10	1	5	4	–	7
Walsh	2	–	–	–	–	–
Ferguson (now Wolves)	1	–	1	–	–	3
Phelan	1	–	2	1	–	4
Martin (now Celtic)	1	–	3	1	–	1
Dublin	1	1	1	–	–	7
Neville	1	–	–	–	–	1
McKee	1	–	–	–	–	–
Sealey (now Blackpool)	–	–	1	–	–	–
Butt	–	–	–	–	–	2
Thornley	–	–	–	–	–	1

(unused substitutes are not included)

GOAL SCORERS 1993–94

	LGE	FA	LC	EC	CS
Cantona	18	4	1	2	–
Giggs	13	1	3	–	–
Hughes	12	4	5	–	1
Sharpe	9	–	2	–	–
Ince	8	1	–	–	–
Kanchelskis	6	3	1	–	–
Keane	5	1	–	2	–
Bruce	3	–	2	2	–
Irwin	2	2	–	–	–
McClair	1	1	4	–	–
Robson	1	1	–	1	–
Dublin	1	–	1	–	–
Pallister	1	–	–	–	–
Own goal	–	–	–	1	–